The
Health
Insurance
Primer

*An Introduction
To How Health
Insurance Works*

America's Health Insurance Plans
Washington, DC 20004

ISBN 1-879143-49-6

CONTENTS

Figures and Tables   v

Foreword   vii

Preface   ix

Acknowledgments   x

About the Authors   xii

1   An Introduction to Insurance   1

2   The Insurance Industry   9

3   Medical Expense Coverage   21

4   Supplemental Coverages   29

5   Disability Income Coverage and
    Long-Term Care Coverage   43

6   Flexible Benefit Plans   53

7   The Insurance Contract   59

8   Provisions of Medical Expense
    Insurance Contracts   67

9   Provisions of Group Medical
    Expense Insurance Contracts   73

10 Provisions of Individual Medical
    Expense Insurance Contracts   81

11 Sales of Group Health Insurance Products   89

12 Sales of Individual Health Insurance Products   99

13 Sales Compensation   107

14 Marketing of Health Insurance Products   113

15 Underwriting of Group Health Insurance   123

16 Underwriting of Individual Health Insurance   143

17 Reinsurance and Reinsurers   155

18 Health Insurance Past, Present, and Future   159

Index   173

AHIP's Courses and Professional Designations   183

AHIP Insurance Education Books   189

The AHIP Insurance Education Program   200

Note on Terminology: All terms are defined in the text as they are introduced. For the page number of the definition of a term, refer to the index.

FIGURES AND TABLES

Chapter 2

Figure 2.1 .... Insurance Status of Workers, Ages 18–64, 1997
Figure 2.2 .... Employment in the Insurance Industry, 1995–1997
Table 2.1 .... Persons with Private Health Insurance, by Type of Insurer, Selected Years

Chapter 3

Table 3.1 .... Surgical Schedule

Chapter 4

Figure 4.1 .... Distribution of Charges for Dental Services, 1997
Figure 4.2 .... Distribution of MedSupp (Medigap) Policies Among 29 Million Persons
Table 4.1 .... Nonscheduled Dental Expense Plan
Table 4.2 .... Standardized Medicare Supplement Policies

Chapter 5

Figure 5.1 .... Individual and Group Association Long-Term Care Policies Sold, 1987–1996

Chapter 6

Table 6.1 .... Modular Format Flexible Benefit Plan
Table 6.2 .... Core-Plus Format Flexible Benefit Plan
Table 6.3 .... Full-Flexible Format Flexible Benefit Plan

Chapter 13

Table 13.1 .... High-Low and Level Commission Schedule
Table 13.2 .... Override Commission Schedule

Chapter 16

Figure 16.1 .... Sample Application for Individual Life and Medical Expense Insurance

Chapter 18

Figure 18.1 .... Enrollment in HMOs, 1980–1997
Figure 18.2 .... Persons with Employer-Sponsored Health Insurance and
Uninsured Persons, 1988–2002

FOREWORD

This book is published by the Insurance Education Program of America's Health Insurance Plans (AHIP).

AHIP is the national association representing nearly 1,300 member companies providing health insurance coverage to more than 200 million Americans. Our member companies offer medical expense insurance, long-term care insurance, disability income insurance, dental insurance, supplemental insurance, stop-loss insurance, and reinsurance to consumers, employers, and public purchasers.

Our goal is to provide a unified voice for the health care financing industry; to expand access to high-quality, cost-effective health care to all Americans; and to ensure Americans' financial security through robust insurance markets, product flexibility, innovation, and an abundance of consumer choice.

The Insurance Education Program aims to be the leader in providing the highest-quality educational materials and services to the health insurance industry and related health care fields. To accomplish this mission, the program seeks to fulfill the following goals:

- provide tools for member company personnel to use in enhancing the quality and efficiency of services to the public;
- provide a career development vehicle for employees and other health care industry professionals; and
- promote general understanding of the role and contribution of the health insurance industry in the financing, administration, and delivery of health care services.

The Insurance Education Program provides the following services:

- a comprehensive course of study in health insurance fundamentals, medical expense insurance, supplemental health insurance, health care management, long-term care insurance, disability income insurance, health care fraud, employee health care benefits, HIPAA, medical management, and customer service in the health care environment;
- certification of educational achievement by examination for all courses;
- programs to recognize accomplishment in the industry and academic communities through course evaluation and certification, which enable participants to obtain academic or continuing education credits; and

- development of educational, instructional, training, and informational materials related to the health insurance and health care industries.

America's Health Insurance Plans (AHIP)
Insurance Education Program
601 Pennsylvania Avenue, NW
South Building, Suite 500
Washington, DC 20004
www.insuranceeducation.org
Email: *mgrant@ahip.org*

PREFACE

The Health Insurance Primer, along with the AHIP book *Health Insurance Nuts and Bolts,* provides an introduction to the underlying concepts of group and individual health insurance, as well as basic information on both the technical and the socioeconomic aspects of health insurance.

Health insurance is a broad array of coverages for sickness or injury, including medical expense insurance, supplemental health insurance, disability income insurance, long-term care insurance, and managed health care. All of these are discussed to some extent in this book, but greatest attention is given to medical expense insurance and disability income insurance, since so many millions of Americans have these coverages. Other books in the AHIP Insurance Education curriculum provide the opportunity to gain a deeper knowledge of other health insurance coverages and of issues of industry-wide concern, such as health care fraud.

This book is based on an earlier Insurance Education book, *Fundamentals of Health Insurance, Part A.* The topics covered are largely the same, but all information has been updated and the text has been substantially reorganized and rewritten to make concepts clearer and information easier to assimilate.

The Health Insurance Primer is accompanied by a study guide. The questions and exercises of the study guide help the reader assimilate the material more easily. The use of the study guide is strongly recommended to those intending to take the AHIP examination.

This book is intended for educational purposes. Its contents are not a statement of policy. The views expressed or suggested in this and all other Insurance Education textbooks are those of the contributing authors or editors and are not necessarily the opinions of AHIP or of its member companies.

Gregory F. Dean JD CLU ChFC LTCP
Executive Director
Insurance Education Program

Terry R. Lowe HIA CLU ChFC FLMI FLHC ACS
General Reviewer and Editor

Michael G. Bell
Editor

ACKNOWLEDGMENTS

Authors

John A. Boni RHU
Lead Product Design Analyst
Physicians Mutual Insurance Company

Elizabeth M. Denning HIA CLU RHU
Vice President of Individual Life Insurance
Guardian Life Insurance Company of America

Marilyn Finley
Director of Product Development
UnumProvident Corporation

Terry R. Lowe HIA CLU ChFC FLMI FLHC ACS
Superintendent, Life/Health Claims
State Farm Insurance

Bernard E. Peskowitz HIA
Administrative Vice President
NYLCare Health Plans, Inc., an Aetna US Healthcare Company

Reviewers

Mary Bailey PhD RN
Professor of Nursing and International Health
Madonna University

John A. Boni RHU
Lead Product Design Analyst
Physicians Mutual Insurance Company

Robyn S.C. Daugherty HIA FLMI
Project Lead/Business Analyst, Department of Pricing and Decision Support
Anthem, Inc.

Karleen Dunkhas
Manager, Product Development and Marketing
Principal Life Insurance Company

Judy Hanson
Compliance Consultant
Disability Reinsurance Management Services, Inc.

Deirdre McKenna, J.D.
Associate Director of Insurance Education
Health Insurance Association of America

Marianne Miller
Private Healthcare Policy Director
America's Health Insurance Plans

Ron Mimick RHU
Product Manager
Mutual of Omaha Insurance Company

Patrice Pirsch HIA MHP CLU FLMI RHU AIRC REBC
Policy Drafting and Compliance Coordinator
Mutual of Omaha Insurance Company

Diana Schuelle
Associate Product Manager, Small Group Marketing
Mutual of Omaha Insurance Company

Lillian M. Simms PhD RN FAAN
Associate Professor of Nursing Emeritus
University of Michigan School of Nursing

Robert Westrick FLMI
Vice President, Underwriting
Employers Reinsurance Corporation

Thomas Wildsmith HIA MHP FSA MAAA CLU ChFC FLMI
Policy Research Actuary
Health Insurance Association of America

General Reviewer and Editor

Terry R. Lowe HIA CLU ChFC FLMI FLHC ACS
Superintendent, Life/Health Claims
State Farm Insurance

Editor

Michael G. Bell

ABOUT THE AUTHORS

John A. Boni has served over 24 years in sales and marketing divisions of the insurance industry—beginning as a field agent and advancing to sales and product management in his company's corporate headquarters. Currently, Boni is Lead Product Design Analyst at Physicians Mutual Insurance Company where his responsibilities include the development of individual and group health and life insurance products.

Elizabeth M. Denning is currently Vice President of Individual Life Insurance at the Guardian Life Insurance Company of America. Prior to her current appointment in January 1999, her 25-year career with Guardian's Individual Disability Division included positions as Second Vice President of Disability Sales and Marketing, Disability Regional Sales Manager in two different regions, Senior Health and Disability Underwriter, and Senior Health and Disability Claims Representative. She has served on HIAA's Individual Insurance Education Subcommittee, the Disability Insurance Training Council of NAHU, the Accident and Health Club of New York, and the Eastern Claims Conference.

Marilyn Finley is a Director of Product Development for UnumProvident Corporation's long-term care division. She is responsible for competitive analysis, design of marketing materials, and development of new and enhanced products. Previously, she held a similar position in the area of individual disability and negotiated regularly with state insurance departments on compliance issues. Prior to that position, Finley supported sales of individual products as a representative of the field and customer services departments.

Terry R. Lowe has enjoyed a 27-year career in the health insurance industry with a concentration in life and individual health insurance claims. He is Superintendent of Life/Health Claims Training and Education for State Farm Insurance and is also a long-time member of the Insurance Education Committee of America's Health Insurance Plans. Lowe has served as an author and editor of numerous health insurance industry publications and is an adjunct professor of insurance and business courses. He has a B.S. in Business Administration and an M.B.A. from Illinois State University.

Bernard E. Peskowitz has enjoyed a long career in compliance and contract development for the insurance industry, working over a period of time for several large companies. Currently, as Administrative Vice President of NYLCare Health Plans, Inc., an Aetna US Healthcare Company, he is responsible for overseeing compliance and contract development for large and small group life, accident and health, and managed indemnity products.

1 AN INTRODUCTION TO INSURANCE

- *Insurance: What It Is and How It Works*
- *Basic Insurance Terms*
- *The Principles of Insurance*
- *The Major Types of Insurance*
- *Needs Met by Health Insurance*

Introduction

We all face hazards in life: illnesses, accidents, natural disasters, criminal acts, and others. These hazards may result in suffering or even death. Some also have economic consequences. For example, an illness may result in thousands of dollars of health care bills. An injury may prevent a person from earning a salary for a period of several years, perhaps for a lifetime. The burning of a home may represent the loss of most of the owner's wealth.

There are four approaches to dealing with the risk of the loss that can result from these hazards. Risk management strategies include:

- **assumption of a risk**, that is, taking no action in advance and suffering the loss if it occurs;
- **elimination of a risk** by avoiding its cause (for example, avoiding the risk of a skiing accident by giving up skiing);
- **reduction of a risk** by taking steps that minimize (but do not eliminate) the likelihood that the hazard will occur (for example, minimizing the risk of illness by exercising and eating well, or minimizing the risk of burglary by installing an alarm system); and
- **transferring all or a part of the risk** to another entity, such as an insurance company, in return for payment of a premium.

This book examines the last risk strategy, insurance, and how one form of it, health insurance, is used to protect against the risk of losses due to illness or injury. This introductory chapter, will explain in general what insurance is and how it works and will describe the major types of insurance.

Insurance: What It Is and How It Works

We all try in different ways to eliminate or minimize risk, but we cannot always prevent bad things from happening. However, we can eliminate or reduce the financial loss that can result. We do this through insurance.

The essence of insurance is spreading the risk of a hazard. That is, a large number of people facing the same kind of risk share the cost of economic loss. Let us suppose, for example, that many people buy fire insurance from a certain insurance company. This means that they each pay a fixed amount of money (a premium) at regular intervals to the company. These premiums form a pool of money from which the company draws to pay for the loss incurred by the few members of the group who actually have a fire. Thus, under this arrangement, everyone in the group of insurance purchasers pays for the loss of the few. But by doing so, each of the purchasers guarantees that he or she will be compensated for any loss from fire. And since the number of people who actually have fires is a very small fraction of the entire group, the premium that the individual pays is very small compared with the amount he or she would lose in a fire.

Thus, insurance can be described as an arrangement of risk management that, for a price, offers the insured an opportunity to share the costs of possible economic loss through an insurance company.

BASIC INSURANCE TERMS

■ An **insurer** (usually an insurance company) sells a **coverage** to a person or organization (the **insured**). A **coverage** is a contractual arrangement that states that the insurer will make a payment to the insured if a certain event occurs. (For example, an insured with fire coverage would be paid in the event of fire.)

■ Such a payment by the insurer to the insured is a **benefit**. A **claim** is a demand by the insured for payment of a benefit.

■ In exchange for coverage, the insured makes payments (usually at regular intervals) to the insurer, known as **premiums**.

■ The legal document that sets the terms of this arrangement is the insurance **policy** or **contract**. The insured is sometimes referred to as the **policyholder**. (Note that there are fine distinctions between **insurance policy** and **insurance contract** and between **policyholder** and **insured.** These will be explained in subsequent chapters.)

The Principles of Insurance

For arrangements like the one described above to work—that is, for insurance to operate successfully—certain conditions must exist. These are:

- uncertainty of loss,
- measurability of loss,
- a large number of insureds,
- a significant size of potential loss, and
- an equitable method of sharing the risk.

Uncertainty of Loss

Insurance is possible only for an event that is unpredictable. If an event is predictable, it makes no sense to buy or sell insurance to protect against it. For example, a person cannot buy a homeowner's insurance policy covering termite infestations for a house that already has termites. Since the payment of repair costs is a certainty in such a case, the insurance company would have to charge the insured the full amount that it would soon be called upon to pay, plus a charge for its services, so that the insured would actually pay more than if she were not insured.

In addition, loss must be uncertain in the sense that it is beyond the control of the insured. The insured must not be able to deliberately cause a loss and be compensated. For this reason, insurance does not cover, for example, self-inflicted injuries.

Measurability of Loss

Measurability of loss means that an insurer must be able to place an exact dollar value on a loss. In many cases this is easy to do—the price of a surgical procedure or hospitalization, or the cost of repairing a car damaged in a collision is known. In other cases the actual dollar amount of loss cannot be determined, but an approximate amount can be agreed upon in advance. For example, it is impossible to put a price tag on the unexpected death of a person. Even if we limit the role of insurance to compensating for the lost earnings of the deceased, it will not be possible to determine just what he would have earned during a normal working life. Therefore, the amount is set in advance. The insured purchases a life insurance policy for a stated amount, which the insurer agrees to pay in case of the insured's death. In either case, whether actual costs or a predetermined amount is used, there must be a basis for determining the exact amount of the benefit due to the insured.

Large Number of Insureds

As explained above, the essence of insurance is spreading risk across large numbers of people. This allows the cost of compensating losses to be shared. It also allows the accurate prediction of the occurrence of losses, which in turn allows the insurer to know how much must be charged in premiums in order to create a pool large enough to cover those losses. A large number of insured makes this prediction possible. An insurance company has no way of knowing if any particular person will suffer a serious and costly illness, but the company can, based on past experience, make a reasonable estimate of the total number of people out of a large group who will incur medical expenses. For example, statistics based on past experience show that of 100,000 persons of a certain age, a certain number will be hospitalized over a given period of time.

Significant Size of Potential Loss

The potential loss must be large enough to make a significant impact on the financial well-being of the insured. No one needs to purchase insurance to cover the cost of a ball-point pen. If it is lost or broken, it can easily be replaced without affecting one's budget. But paying a hospital bill of several thousand dollars could bankrupt many people. Similarly, many people may never recover financially if the most valuable thing they own—a house, a car, or their earning power—is destroyed. It is against catastrophic losses that insurance is most necessary.

Some people want to have insurance to cover even a $50 loss. For someone living on a very low income, even this seemingly insignificant amount may be difficult to pay. Insurers can and do provide insurance for people who want coverage for low-cost items, but it is not a very efficient use of insurance. The insurer must collect funds from its insureds that are sufficient to cover not only the losses insured against, but also its own expenses of handling the transaction and a reasonable profit. It costs the insurer almost as much to pay a $50 claim as to pay a claim many times larger. The efficient use of premium dollars is to purchase insurance to cover potential losses that will significantly affect the insured's financial status.

Equitable Sharing

proportionate

Insurance is based on sharing risk—that is, sharing the cost of losses. Equitable sharing means that the risk is shared in a fair way. If everyone has the same potential loss, then premiums should be the same for all. However, if some people have a greater potential loss, they should pay more. In the case of fire insurance for example, a person with a more expensive house will have a greater loss in case of fire than others with less expensive houses and will be compensated more. Therefore, that person should pay higher premiums.

A Clarification of "Risk"

The term "risk" is used in different ways in the insurance industry. In general, it means the financial loss that is insured against. More specifically it refers to the known or probable cost of compensating for that loss. It is also sometimes used more loosely to refer to the person being insured or to the hazard insured against. Thus in fire insurance, "risk" normally refers to the risk that the insurance company will have to pay for damage by fire to the property of one of its insureds, but the word may also be used for fire itself or for a holder of the company's fire insurance policy.

In addition, a distinction must be made between speculative risk and pure risk.

- **Speculative risk** occurs when a person invests money in a business or in securities such as stocks. If the business fails or the securities decline in value, the investor suffers a loss. If the business does well or the value of the securities increases, the investor gains money. The investor accepts the risk of loss in return for the possibility of gain.
- In **pure risk** there is no possibility of gain. There is only the possibility of no loss, or a loss due to unforeseen and unexpected hazards beyond the control of the one for whom the risk exists. This is the kind of risk that insurance is designed to cover.

The Major Types of Insurance

There are four major types of insurance policies, which are usually grouped into two categories: life and health, and property and casualty. In addition, these four types of insurance can be bought on an individual or group basis.

Individual and Group Insurance

In individual insurance, a private person buys coverage. He is the policyholder and he (and in some cases his dependents) receives coverage. In group insurance, a group such as an association or a union buys insurance for its members, or more commonly a business buys insurance for its employees. The members of the group or the employees receive coverage, but the policyholder is the group or the business. Members or employees may pay all or part of the premiums, but they do so through the policyholder.

Life and Health Insurance

Life insurance and health insurance are usually grouped together because both are **personal insurance**; in other words, they cover particular persons and pay benefits in the event those persons die or suffer an illness or accident. Personal insurance can be bought by individuals for themselves or by groups or employers for individuals.

Life Insurance

Life insurance pays benefits in the event of the death of the insured. Benefits are paid to a person designated by the insured, the **beneficiary**.

There are several types of life insurance policies:

Ordinary life insurance is the most widely purchased and is available in two subtypes: permanent and term.

- **Permanent life insurance** offers protection for the entire life of the insured and is also known as **whole life insurance**. Permanent life insurance policies build up cash value and are used by many people as a way to save money.
- **Term life insurance** policies generally offer protection for a specified period of time and most do not build up cash value.

There are two other types of life insurance:

- **Credit life insurance** may be used to pay down the balance of loans that may be outstanding if a borrower dies.
- **Annuity contracts** guarantee payments to a designated party for a specific time period or for life. Annuities often are used to provide retirement income or income for a surviving spouse.

Health Insurance

Health insurance pays benefits in the event of sickness or injury. It is also known as accident and health insurance or sickness and accident insurance. Health insurance covers many health care expenses, including medical, hospital, surgical, and dental expenses. Health insurance also may compensate for loss of income if the sickness or injury makes the insured unable to work.

Property and Casualty Insurance

Property insurance and casualty insurance are grouped together because they are not personal insurance. They cover property and events, not persons. These policies are bought by both businesses and individuals. More than 3,000 insurance companies in the United States sell some form of property and casualty insurance.

Property insurance pays benefits to compensate for loss of and damage to homes and their contents, commercial and industrial buildings, equipment, furniture, fixtures, inventories, business records, supplies, automobiles, and other physical items. Two types of property losses are covered:

- **Direct:** the lost value of stolen, damaged, lost, or destroyed property.
- **Indirect:** expenses incurred because of the loss, such as the expense of temporary housing, loss of rental income, and loss of profits.

Casualty insurance protects the insured against costs arising from legal liabilities. When another person (not the insured) suffers injury or damage and the insured is legally liable, casualty insurance reimburses for the costs that the insured is required to pay. An example is automobile liability insurance—if the insured is in an accident and it is determined that he is liable for damage to the other party's car, his liability coverage pays the costs of repair. (Any repair costs for the insured's own car is paid for by the property insurance part of his automobile insurance policy.) A physician's malpractice insurance is another form of casualty insurance.

Needs Met By Health Insurance

The costs resulting from adverse changes in health can be so great that very few people could afford to pay for them themselves. Therefore, almost everybody needs health insurance. Health insurance helps people by:

- reimbursing for medical expenses;
- providing a set amount of income replacement; and/or
- providing a lump-sum payment for losses.

The Need for Medical Expense Insurance

The cost of medical care can reach substantial amounts. Hospital charges well over $10,000 can be incurred in a few days. Surgery, including hospital and doctors' bills, easily can reach or exceed $20,000. The expenses of a hospital stay of 30 days or more can be devastating. Medical expense insurance, discussed in Chapter Three, helps pay these costs.

The Need for Supplemental Insurance

Typically, some of the costs of hospitalization and medical care are not covered by medical expense insurance and must be borne by the insured. Supplemental health insurance can help pay these costs. In addition, there are supplemental coverages for other types of care (such as dental and vision care) that medical expense insurance does not usually cover at all. Supplemental coverage is discussed in Chapter Four.

The Need for Disability Income Insurance

Working adults need disability income insurance to protect against the possibility of not being able to earn a full salary because of sickness or injury. Assume that a 30-year-old person is injured and not able to work, and that the injury does not shorten his life span. If this person's monthly earnings are $3,000, the salary loss each year is $36,000. Even assuming no pay increases, the total amount of earnings lost between age 30 and the normal retirement age of 65 will be $1,260,000. This is certainly an amount worth insuring.

The Need for Long-Term Care Insurance

Charges for skilled care in a nursing home can reach or exceed $40,000 per year. Care provided at home by a nurse or home health aide is also quite expensive. Long-term care insurance can help meet these expenses.

There is a great need for long-term care insurance. A survey estimates that one in five Americans over age 50 is at risk of needing long-term care services during the next 12 months. And the need for long-term care is increasing. The likelihood of needing long-term care insurance increases with age, and the U.S. population is aging. In addition, smaller families, divorce, and the geographic dispersal of families may result in more older people being in situations where there are no family caregivers and paid professional care is the only alternative.

Disability income insurance and long-term care insurance are discussed in Chapter Five.

Summary

Insurance is a way of protecting ourselves from the financial losses caused by life's hazards. By paying small amounts on a regular basis we avoid paying a very large amount unexpectedly. There are many kinds of insurance coverages that protect against a variety of hazards. This book will examine health insurance, describe the various types of health coverages, and explain how they work.

2 THE INSURANCE INDUSTRY

- *The Importance of the Life and Health Insurance Industry in the United States*
- *Types of Organizations*
- *Stock and Mutual Companies*
- *Other Organizations Providing Protection*
- *The Canadian Life and Health Insurance Industry*

Introduction

As shown in the previous chapter, insurance fills an important need—it helps people and businesses protect themselves from the uncertainties of life. In addition, because of the assets it holds and the number of people it employs, the insurance industry is an important part of our economy. This chapter will examine the impact of this industry and the kinds of companies that constitute it.

In this chapter, we will in some cases treat life and health insurance together. This is because a large proportion (approximately 95 percent in the United States) of all health insurance business is conducted by life insurance companies, and some statistics cover the two types of insurance together. Also, the chapter will describe the Canadian insurance industry separately, as it is different from the American industry in important ways.

The Importance of the Life and Health Insurance Industry in the United States

- **Protection provided.** The insurance industry provides protection against illness and accident to most Americans. In 1997, about 70 percent of the population had some form of private (non-governmental) health insurance. By far the predominant form of health insurance is employer-sponsored group insurance. (See Figure 2.1.)

- **Number of companies.** About 800 life insurance companies (out of about 1,500 life insurance companies in the United States) also sell health insurance, and as noted above, they account for about 95 percent of business. An additional 150 property and casualty insurance companies sell health insurance as well.
- **Assets.** Current assets of the life and health insurance industry are over $2.5 trillion. These assets are split between government securities, corporate securities (such as stocks and bonds), mortgages, real estate, and policy loans.
- **Employment.** The insurance industry as a whole employs more than 2.2 million people in the United States. Of these, about 900,000 work in the life and health insurance field. Most of these employees work directly for insurance companies. Others work for insurance agencies, brokerage operations, or other service organizations such as rating bureaus. Still others are independent claims adjusters, appraisers, and loss control service providers. (See Figure 2.2.)

Types of Organizations

Health insurance is provided mostly by commercial insurance companies. These include stock companies and mutual companies. In addition, other entities provide different kinds of protection against illness and injury and so shape the environment that insurance companies operate in. These entities include:

- Blue Cross/Blue Shield plans (As will be explained, these are not strictly speaking insurance companies, although they are very similar.)
- Managed care organizations
- Self-insured groups
- Fraternal societies
- Government programs

Stock and Mutual Companies

Commercial insurance companies are divided between stock companies and mutual companies. In 1997, 93 percent of life and health insurance companies in business were stock companies. However, mutual companies account for approximately half of the life insurance in force, as many of the largest life insurance companies are mutual.

FIGURE 2.1

Insurance Status of Workers, Ages 18–64, 1997

There are 122.7 million
wage and salary earners
(public and private sectors combined).

There are 12.1 million
self-employed
persons.

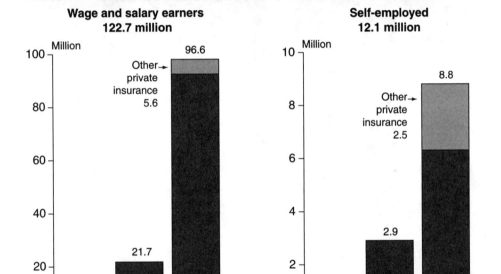

**Wage and salary earners
122.7 million**

**Self-employed
12.1 million**

Note: Numbers do not always total, because a worker's status may change during a year.
Source: Employee Benefit Research Institute (EBRI) estimates of the March 1998 Current Population Survey.

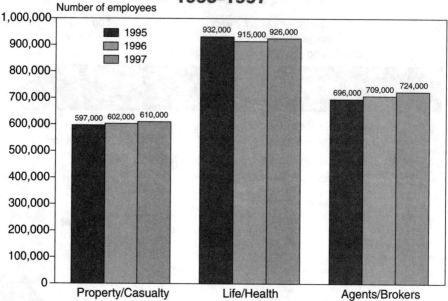

FIGURE 2.2

Employment in the Insurance Industry, 1995–1997

Source: Bureau of Labor Statistics, U.S. Dept. of Labor.

Stock Insurance Companies

The majority of large companies in most fields of business are stock companies. In a stock company, people may purchase shares of the company's stock. These are literally "shares" of ownership of the company—the stockholders of the company are each part-owners of the company. The stockholders control the company through stockholder voting and receive the profits of the company. The percentage of ownership that one person holds is determined by the number of shares of stock that person owns compared with the total number of shares that have been issued. The stockholders share in the earnings of the company by receiving periodic (usually quarterly) payments called dividends. The size of the dividend is dependent on the number of shares an individual owns and the most recent performance of the company.

A stock insurance company is formed to earn money for its stockholders by selling insurance. This means that a stock company, when determining premium rates, must take into consideration the need to realize a profit. However, this profit, as

TABLE 2.1

Persons with Private Health Insurance, by Type of Insurer, Selected Years (Millions)

	1991	1992	1993	1994	1995	1996
All insurers	181.0	180.7	180.9	182.2	185.3	187.5
Insurance companies (net)	78.0	76.6	74.7	75.8	76.6	75.4
Group	83.3	82.1	80.9	82.4	83.3	84.2
Fully insured	36.2	33.8	33.3	36.8	37.1	36.2
ASO	35.3	35.9	37.2	37.4	39.9	40.7
MPP	11.8	12.4	10.4	8.2	6.3	7.0
Individual	9.9	8.5	7.4	7.0	7.0	7.0
Blue Cross Blue Shield	68.1	67.5	65.9	65.2	65.6	67.6
Self-insured	54.8	56.5	60.5	61.8	61.0	62.0
HMO	38.7	41.4	45.2	51.1	59.1	66.8
Blue Cross Blue Shield	4.7	5.8	6.7	7.6	8.8	12.6
Insurance companies	6.0	6.1	6.5	7.3	8.5	12.7
Other	28.0	29.5	32.0	36.2	41.8	41.5

Source: Health Insurance Association of America, Estimates.

a percentage of the premium, may be very small. Most insurance companies target about a 3 percent annual profit margin.

When a new stock insurance company is formed, state regulations require that the company have a certain amount of capital and a certain amount of surplus funds. (See box.) In most states, the minimum capital required for a stock company planning to write health insurance falls in the range of $100,000 to $1,000,000. Requirements for surplus funds may be as much as 200 percent of the minimum capital. Well-financed stock insurance companies have an initial capital and surplus considerably in excess of the required minimums.

CAPITAL, SURPLUS, AND LIABILITY

Capital is the money needed to start a business. A **surplus**, in the context of insurance, is the amount by which the value of an insurer's assets exceeds its liabilities. A **liability** is the probable cost of meeting a financial obligation. In the case of an insurance company, liabilities would normally include paying claims on the insurance it has written, plus any other financial obligations the company has assumed.

Mutual Insurers

A mutual company is different from most publicly-owned companies. It has no stockholders. The ownership and control of a mutual insurance company is held by its policyholders. Each policyholder is eligible to vote in elections of the company's board of directors and has one vote, regardless of the number of policies owned or the amount of insurance purchased.

Mutual insurers do not seek profit as does a stock insurer. However, in determining premium rates, they too must charge more than the bare amount needed to cover costs. This is because they must set aside a surplus. This surplus serves as a margin of safety, a guarantee of the solvency and continuity of the organization despite any conceivable adverse circumstances. Therefore, the size of the surplus is a measure of the financial strength and stability of the insurer. Also, if a company wants to grow by writing new business (that is, by selling additional insurance policies), it must have a surplus sufficient to cover the new obligations this new business will entail. Therefore, the size of a company's surplus partially determines its potential for growth.

For these reasons, mutual insurers usually try to have some degree of growth in their surplus. They do this by adding an allowance for addition to surplus in determining premium rates, just as stock companies add an allowance for profit. And although mutual companies do not exist for the purpose of paying dividends, as does a stock company, if a company's surplus has reached its optimum size, excess amounts may be returned to the company's policyholders as dividends.

When a new mutual insurance company is formed, state regulations require that it have a minimum number of applications for insurance accompanied by premiums and a minimum amount of surplus funds. In some states, the requirements to form a mutual insurer are so strict that it is now virtually impossible to form a new mutual company. Almost all mutual insurers that now exist were organized originally as stock companies and later mutualized. (See below for how this is done.)

Changing Ownership Type

A company can choose to change its ownership from a stock insurance company to a mutual insurance company and vice versa. State governments impose a number of legal and regulatory requirements that must be met in making such a change. The process can be lengthy and expensive.

Most changes today are from mutual to stock. This is called **demutualization.** Demutualization gives a company several advantages:

• **Greater ability to raise capital.** Stock companies can raise money by selling new shares of stock. (That is, people give the company money in exchange for becoming additional part-owners of the company, or existing shareholders give money to increase their share of ownership.)

- **Greater ability to acquire other companies.** The ability to raise money mentioned above gives stock companies an advantage in buying other companies. Regulations also put mutual companies at a disadvantage in this area— mutual companies are limited in the ways that they can use their surplus, and if a mutual company buys a stock company, the purchased company is subject to mutual regulations.
- **Greater flexibility in attracting top-level employees.** Stock companies can offer shares of company stock or stock options as part of the overall compensation package, which can be very attractive to potential executives.
- **Reduction in the tax burden.** Recent changes in the corporate income tax structure have placed a potentially higher tax burden on mutual insurance companies.

The disadvantages of demutualization generally lie with the cost of accomplishing such a conversion, the difficulty in making an equitable distribution of the mutual company's surplus among its policy owners, and the complications in the process due to the great variation in applicable laws from state to state.

Conversion from stock to mutual was once common, but it happens with much less frequency today. The main advantage of **mutualization** is that it gives the company's management more control over the operations of the company by freeing it from the demands of the stockholders. Mutualization is usually accomplished by using surplus funds to buy all stock from the shareholders.

Other Organizations Providing Protection

Blue Cross and Blue Shield Plans

The Blue Cross and Blue Shield plans were not begun as insurance companies. However, from the beginning they have filled many of the same functions as insurers, and more recently they have evolved to become more like insurers.

The first Blues were established in the 1930s. They were nonprofit organizations sponsored by local hospital groups (Blue Cross) or physician groups (Blue Shield). The Blues were prepaid service plans, not insurance companies. That is, subscribers of the Blues did not receive indemnification (compensation) to pay for medical expenses that they incurred; rather, in return for making monthly payments, they received certain specified medical services when they needed them directly from physicians or hospitals that were members of the plans. Thus, although this system was not strictly insurance, it served the same purpose.

The Blues enjoyed some advantages over insurers, such as favorable reimbursement agreements with hospitals and doctors (since the Blues *were* in a sense the doctors and hospitals) and preferential tax status (since they were not-for-profit organizations). On the other hand, because of their professional, nonprofit status, the Blues were expected to serve the community in a way insurance companies were not. For example, Blues often had to accept as members people whom commercial insurers would not accept. Blues also were often required to practice **community rating**, that is, charging everyone in the community the same rate, even if the characteristics of certain individuals or groups made them greater risks.

In recent years, Blue Cross and Blue Shield plans have changed in ways that have made them less distinct from insurance companies. As a result, in 1986 Congress withdrew the Blue Cross/Blue Shield exemption from federal income tax. Also, some states have required plans to pay more in state, local, and premium taxes.

Some plans have undergone more radical changes. Some have become mutual insurance companies. Others have become stock companies. Still others have subsidiary operations that are stock companies, offering insurance or managed care products.

Mergers have also had an impact on the Blues. Plans have merged, sometimes across state lines, so that the 100 independent plans that existed in the 1980s have been reduced to about 50. Some plans have also merged with commercial insurers.

An advantage that the Blues continue to enjoy is their national trade association, the Blue Cross and Blue Shield Association. This association markets the plans on a national level, contracting with large national employer groups and the federal government on behalf of the local plans. The association, so that it can meet its obligations to these entities, can require the participation and cooperation of the local plans. The association also licenses the local plans to use the Blue Cross and Blue Shield names and symbols and requires compliance with certain standards of organization, operations, products, and services.

Managed Care Organizations

Managed care organizations (MCOs) include various types of health maintenance organizations (HMOs), preferred provider organizations (PPOs), point-of-service (POS) plans, and other entities. As with Blue Cross/Blue Shield plans, there was once a clear distinction between managed care and health insurance, but that distinction has become blurred. Early types of MCOs, such as staff-model and group-model HMOs, differed from insurance plans in that they did not simply compensate their members for the cost of medical care—rather they provided that care through physicians employed in the HMO's own facilities or through the HMO's network of contracted physicians. These HMOs also differed from traditional insurance plans in that they did not compensate for any care provided outside their facilities or networks. A few HMOs still operate in this way, but many other types of MCOs have developed that give their members more freedom in choosing their health care providers. At the same time, insurance companies have adopted many of the techniques developed by MCOs to improve the quality and cost-effectiveness of health care. Finally, although early MCOs were typically not-for-profit organizations, many are now for-profit businesses, and some are owned by insurance companies and Blue Cross/Blue Shield plans. As a result, it is no longer possible to draw a clear line between the coverages offered by MCOs and those offered by insurance companies. Instead there is now a continuum of coverages, with traditional managed care at one end, traditional insurance at the other, and in the middle a variety of coverages combining the features of both approaches. These innovative coverages are provided by both MCOs and insurance companies.

Managed care is discussed in detail in *Health Insurance Nuts and Bolts: An Introduction to Health Insurance Operations*. The HIAA Insurance Education curriculum also includes a three-part course in managed care.

Self-Insured Groups

A growing number of group health insurance plans are self-insured. A large company or union, instead of purchasing coverage for its employees or members from an insurer, establishes its own health insurance program and pays claims out of its own funds. This allows the company to cut out the middleman and improve cash flow, and it also has some tax and regulatory advantages.

Despite the fact that they do not purchase insurance, such groups provide a market for insurers. Insurers can process claims and provide other administrative services in return for a fee. This is known as an **administrative services only (ASO)** arrangement. In addition, some groups are only partially self-insured—an employer takes responsibility for the group's expected level of claims and purchases insurance to cover claims above this expected level. This is known as a **minimum premium plan (MPP)**.

Fraternal Societies

Some fraternal societies offer insurance, although they are not a major part of the industry. Fraternal societies are not businesses, but rather social organizations, and they provide insurance only to their own members. Separate laws govern the insurance activities of fraternal societies, but these laws have the same purpose as those governing mutual and stock companies: to ensure that the organization has the financial capacity to meet all of its insurance commitments.

Government Programs

Various government programs pay for health care.

- **Medicare** serves persons over age 65 and others with certain disabilities.
- **Medicaid** serves a portion of the indigent population as well as certain categories of the medically needy.
- **State workers' compensation programs** pay benefits to those suffering from work-related injuries and diseases.
- **Military programs** provide health care benefits for active service persons, veterans, and the dependents of both.

The Canadian Life and Health Insurance Industry

As in the United States, in Canada life and health insurance is a major business with an important impact on the national economy.

- **Protection provided.** Although Canadians largely rely on government programs to pay for most medical expenses, at the end of 1998 commercial insurers were providing extended health care insurance to 14.9 million people, dental insurance to 7.5 million, and long-term disability insurance to 6.3 million.
- **Number of companies.** At the end of 1997, 109 life insurance companies and 51 property and casualty insurance companies were providing health insurance in Canada.
- **Assets.** The total assets held in Canada on behalf of Canadian life and health insurance policyholders amounted to $227.2 billion (1998). Stocks and bonds are major components of the Canadian life and health insurance industry's total asset portfolio. The industry also is a major source of financing for the national and provincial governments. Government bonds and treasury bills accounted for 23 percent of the industry's total assets, with the majority held at the federal level.
- **Employment.** In 1998 approximately 105,000 people worked in the life and health insurance business in Canada.

Differences Between the Canadian and U.S. Industries

The Canadian insurance industry differs in several important ways from the U.S. insurance industry, mostly because of the different roles of the two countries' governments. Major differences are:

- In Canada, a government-administered health care system dominates the health care field, whereas the United States does not have such a system.
- Canada has a higher proportion of mutual insurance companies to stock insurance companies than the United States.

- The Canadian government does not regulate the insurance industry as heavily as in the United States; rather, the Canadian system is highly self-regulated.
- In Canada, regulatory responsibility in the field of insurance is shared by the federal and provincial governments. In the United States, it is primarily the responsibility of the states.

Government Health Insurance in Canada

Each Canadian province provides all its residents with a comprehensive program of hospitalization and medical expense coverage. These universal plans are funded by a combination of grants from provincial and federal governments, direct or general tax revenues, and, in most provinces, a small premium. Private medical expense insurance is available and may be used to meet needs not met by government coverage.

The Importance of Mutual Companies

Mutual companies play a greater role in the Canadian insurance industry as a result of government policy. The Canadian government has been concerned about Canadian companies being taken over by foreign companies. Since mutual companies do not have stock that foreign companies can buy, they are much more difficult to acquire than stock companies. Therefore, the Canadian government has encouraged stock companies to mutualize. This policy has been a success, as many Canadian companies have successfully avoided takeovers by foreign companies by the process of mutualization.

Regulation

The regulatory responsibility and supervisory control of the Canadian insurance industry is shared between the federal and provincial governments.

The provinces have the sole responsibility for legislation regarding:

- the form of the insurance contract;
- advertising and consumer protection; and
- the licensing and regulation of agents, brokers, and adjusters.

The licensing of insurers and other regulatory functions are divided between the federal and provincial governments.

- All insurers must be licensed by every province in which they operate. The exception is Nova Scotia, which has requested that the federal government license and supervise insurance companies operating in that province.
- All federally incorporated Canadian insurers and all non-Canadian insurers doing business in Canada must have a federal license in addition to their provincial

license or licenses. Other companies have no obligation to get a federal license, but many voluntarily do so because of the prestige attached to federal registry.

As part of the licensing process, the provinces require the filing of documents of incorporation. Once licensed, the insurer must file an annual statement showing its business in the province. The provinces also supervise and assume responsibility for inspections relating to the solvency of insurers that are not also registered with the federal government.

The federal government inspects insurance companies licensed by it and administers legislation concerning the deposits, solvency, and valuation of assets and liabilities of these companies.

Summary

In both the United States and Canada, the health insurance industry is an important part of the economy, due to the number of people it employs and the assets it holds. It is also important in terms of the number of people it protects. This protection is provided by several different types of organizations, including stock and mutual companies, Blue Cross/Blue Shield plans, and managed care organizations. In Canada, government programs play a larger role in paying for health care, and as a result the Canadian and American industries differ in some ways.

3 MEDICAL EXPENSE COVERAGE

- *Hospital-Surgical Insurance*
- *Exclusions and Limitations*
- *Major Medical Insurance*
- *Deductibles, Coinsurance, and Overall Maximums*

Introduction

The costs of surgery and hospitalization are the greatest health-related expenses that most people encounter. Medical expense coverage is designed to protect the insured against financial losses by reimbursing for these costs. The two major types of medical expense coverage are hospital-surgical insurance (basic medical expense insurance) and major medical insurance. There are two types of major medical insurance: supplemental and comprehensive. All of these coverages are offered on both a group and an individual basis.

Hospital-Surgical Insurance

Hospital-surgical insurance is also known as basic medical expense insurance. A hospital-surgical policy stipulates and defines certain medical expenses and agrees to make specified payments for those expenses. There is a wide variety of policies. Policies differ in the expenses they cover and in the amount they pay for a given expense.

Expenses Covered

Expenses that may be covered include the following:

- **Hospital room and board,** including general nursing care.
- **Miscellaneous hospital charges.** These are for services and supplies (other than room and board and general nursing care) furnished during a hospital stay, including laboratory services, X-ray examinations, medicines and drugs,

surgical dressings, operating room expenses, and ambulance service. Also usually included are the services of hospital-employed professionals such as pathologists, radiologists, and anesthetists.

- **Surgical charges.** These are the fees charged by a surgeon for surgical operations (including surgery performed on both an inhospital and outpatient basis).
- **Physician's inhospital charges.** These are the fees charged by a physician for nonsurgical treatment during hospital confinement.
- **Charges for outpatient services,** including outpatient diagnostic X-ray services and other outpatient lab services.
- **Charges for maternity services.**

Benefits Paid

A hospital-surgical policy sets or limits the amount of benefit that will be paid for each expense. A dollar amount may be fixed in advance or the benefit may be defined as the usual and customary charges for a given service. In addition, some policies have an overall maximum benefit, a limit on the total amount they will pay to the insured.

Typical benefits for common expenses are the following:

- **Hospital room and board.** Historically, hospital-surgical policies have paid a daily maximum (for example, $100 a day), the amount varying with different policies to reflect the fact that room and board charges vary from place to place. However, most insurers have moved away from the concept of fixed room and board maximums and now reimburse for whatever the hospital charges for a semiprivate room.
- **Surgical charges.** A surgical schedule is typically used. (See Table 3.1.) It lists cash allowances for common surgical procedures up to a maximum amount, or it may express the maximum allowed for each procedure as a percentage of the overall policy maximum benefit.
  In addition, most policies require a second surgical opinion for optional inpatient and outpatient surgery. If the patient has optional surgery without seeking a second opinion, the plan may not pay the surgical benefit or may reimburse the surgical benefit at a lower level.
- **Physician's inhospital charges.** Policies state a maximum amount that will be paid for each visit by a physician. They also usually limit the number of visits that will be covered during one period of hospitalization.
- **Outpatient diagnostic X-ray and lab charges.** The maximum amount payable may be limited to $200 or $500 for any one illness or injury. However, some policies allow reimbursement up to the overall maximum benefit, which is often several thousand dollars.
- **Maternity expenses.** Some plans make maternity coverage optional or cover only part of maternity expenses. However, some states have legislation mandat-

TABLE 3.1

Surgical Schedule

Cardiovascular system	Percentage of maximum surgical benefit
Repair of heart valve, mitral	32.0
Aortic, pulmonic or tricuspid	50.0
Catheterization of heart, independent procedure	4.0
Double valve procedure, replacement and/or repair by valvuloplasty or replacement	70.0
Triple valve procedure, replacement and/or repair	80.0
Excision and graft, thoracic aorta	48.0
Repair aneurysm of aorta	56.0
Aortography	2.7
Coronary angioplasty (endarterectomy, arterial implantation, or anastomosis, with bypass)	60.0

ing that maternity benefits be covered in full just like any other illness or health condition.

Exclusions and Limitations

In addition to language specifying what medical expenses will be reimbursed and to what extent, policies also contain exclusions and limitations. Exclusions state what expenses the insurer will not reimburse. They also establish that under certain circumstances the insurer will not pay benefits for expenses that would usually be reimbursed. (For example, a policy might normally pay benefits for injuries, but not for self-inflicted injuries.) Limitations state expenses for which the insurer will pay benefits but at a reduced level, as well as circumstances under which the insurer will pay reduced benefits.

Medical expense plans commonly exclude or limit payment for **preexisting conditions**—medical conditions that existed before the insurance policy went into effect. As was explained in Chapter One, without uncertainty insurance does not make economic sense for either the insurer or the insured. If the insurer knows with certainty that a potential insured will incur certain expenses, in order to offer coverage it would have to charge the insured as a premium the full cost of those expenses plus administrative costs. Neither the insured nor the insurer would gain anything by the arrangement. Insurance is a means of dealing with possible future events, not events that have already occurred or are certain to occur.

Most group medical expense policies only exclude conditions that the insured has been treated for during a certain period of time before the policy takes effect, often three or six months. This is known as the **look-back period**. For example, if the look-back period of a policy is six months, and an insured has previously suffered from asthma but was not treated for it during the six months before coverage began, the insured's asthma would not be excluded as a preexisting condition. In addition, under some group policies once someone has been insured for a certain period of time or meets other criteria, preexisting conditions are covered on the same basis as any other condition.

Individual medical expense policies operate in a similar way, but look-back periods can be as long as three years, and exclusions may last longer than for group policies.

Many states place restrictions on the use of exclusions for preexisting conditions. In addition, the federal **Health Insurance Portability and Accountability Act of 1996 (HIPAA)** limits their use in various ways. For example, HIPAA prohibits treating pregnancy as a preexisting condition in group policies. Also, under HIPAA a group policy's look-back period cannot be more than six months, and the period during which benefits are not paid for a preexisting condition cannot be more than 12 months. Moreover, when a person moves from one group plan to another, this 12-month period is reduced by the amount of time she was covered by the previous plan. (For example, if the person previously had group health insurance for seven months, the preexisting condition exclusion can only last five months; if the person was previously covered for 12 months or more, there can be no preexisting condition exclusion.) This reduction occurs provided the gap between coverage under the two plans is not greater than 63 days.

Medical expense plans also commonly exclude or limit benefits for the following:

- **Intentionally self-inflicted injuries.** As explained in Chapter One, the principle of uncertainty requires that the insured not collect benefits from hazards that he directly causes himself.
- **Dental care, vision care and eyeglasses, and hearing aids.** These expenses are covered by various supplemental insurance policies. (See Chapter Four.)
- **Custodial care (long-term nursing care).** This is provided by long-term care insurance. (See Chapter Five.)
- **Occupational accidents and sicknesses.** These are covered by state workers' compensation programs.
- **Elective medical services.** These are services not necessary to alleviate illness or injury, such as cosmetic surgery or treatment for sexual dysfunction. Routine health examinations or periodic check-ups may also be considered elective medical services.
- **Care received from any government agency.** Since the insured does not actually pay for these services, he does not receive benefits.
- **Military service and war.** This includes all illnesses and injuries sustained during full-time active military duty or during war, declared or undeclared, including armed aggression or resistance to aggression. This exclusion is intended to prevent the insurer from making promises it cannot keep. If a war occured there would be so many claims that the insurer would not have the resources to pay them all.
- **Mental or nervous disorders.**

- **Transportation (except for local ambulance service).**
- **Charges not found to be usual and customary charges.**

Major Medical Insurance

We have covered hospital-surgical insurance first, as it is the basic form of medical expense insurance. However, major medical insurance is now far more common. The two coverages are generally similar, but major medical policies differ from hospital-surgical policies in the following ways:

- Major medical generally provides much greater coverage. Typically, more kinds of expenses are covered, benefits for specific expenses are less limited, and the overall maximum benefit is usually very high or even unlimited.
- Hospital-surgical plans, while limiting the amount of a benefit, usually pay all of the specified amount. Major medical plans, on the other hand, require the insured to pay part of the expenses through a deductible and coinsurance (explained below).

There are two kinds of major medical insurance:

- **Supplemental major medical** supplements a basic (hospital-surgical) plan—that is, it provides coverage for expenses not covered by the basic plan and adds additional benefits for those expenses that are covered but in a limited way.
- **Comprehensive major medical** combines in one plan all the coverage provided by a hospital-surgical plan and a supplemental major medical plan. This results in simplicity of plan design and the avoidance of overlapping coverages.

Comprehensive major medical is more common than supplemental.

It should be clarified that supplemental major medical insurance, despite its name, is not one of the forms of insurance usually referred to as supplemental coverages (or supplemental insurance). These coverages, which will be discussed in Chapter Four, supplement a broad-based plan of medical expense insurance that provides coverage for most necessary medical expenses. Supplemental major medical insurance, on the other hand, is combined with basic hospital-surgical coverage to form such a broad-based plan.

Covered Expenses, Exclusions, and Limitations

Major medical policies, like basic medical expense policies, specify the services and supplies that are covered and exclude and limit other expenses. Covered, excluded, and limited expenses are roughly the same as those listed for hospital-surgical insurance. However, as stated above, in general major medical covers more expenses and pays greater benefits.

Deductibles

A deductible is a portion of covered medical expenses that the insured must pay. For example, if a policy has a $500 deductible for medical expenses, and an insured incurs medical expenses of $850, the insured must pay the first $500 and the insurer will pay the remaining $350 (or more precisely, all of the remaining expenses that are covered by the policy). "Deductible" is specifically defined as the amount of covered benefit that must be incurred and paid by the insured before benefits become payable by the insurer.

Let us suppose that the insured incurred an expense of only $300 dollars. In this case, the insured must pay all of the $300, because this amount is less than the $500 deductible. However, a deductible is usually **cumulative**, meaning that the $300 paid by the insured counts toward the $500 total deductible. If the insured incurs another expense, he will only have to pay the first $200, at which point the $500 deductible will be satisfied, and the insurer will pay the rest of covered expenses.

The **accumulation period** of a deductible is usually the calendar year (January 1 to December 31). This means that at the beginning of the year, the deductible is once again $500 (to use our example), and the insured must begin again to satisfy the deductible. However, this also means that the insured will not have to pay more than $500 in deductible during each calendar year.

If a coverage does not require a deductible, it is said to offer **first-dollar coverage**—that is, it pays benefits beginning with the first dollar of expense.

The deductible has two purposes:

- It discourages the insured from unnecessarily incurring costs, since she will have to pay a portion of these costs.
- It eliminates small claims and the expense of handling them.

In both cases the insurer's costs are reduced, which allows the insurer to keep the price of premiums down.

Two types of deductible are common in comprehensive major medical plans:

- **All cause deductible.** In a policy with an all cause deductible, all expenses incurred for all illnesses and accidents apply to one deductible. The accumulation period is almost universally the calendar year. The all cause deductible has the advantages of being simple to administer and easy for the insured to understand.

- **Per cause deductible.** In a policy with a per cause deductible, there is a separate deductible for each illness or accident. The accumulation period for each cause starts on the date of the first expense for that cause and normally ends one or two years later. At that point, if the insured is still incurring expenses for the same cause, the deductible must be satisfied again and a new accumulation period begins.

The all cause deductible is much more common that the per cause deductible.

Two types of deductibles are used by supplemental major medical plans to coordinate benefits with the basic plans that they supplement:

- **Corridor deductible.** With a corridor deductible, when medical expenses exceed the benefits of the basic plan, before the supplemental plan pays benefits a deductible must be satisfied. As an example, let us suppose that an insured's basic policy pays $1,000 for X-rays, and his supplemental major medical policy pays all additional X-ray expenses, but with a $500 corridor deductible. If the insured is charged $2,000 for X-rays, the basic policy will pay the first $1,000, the insured will pay a $500 corridor deductible, and the supplemental plan will pay the remaining $500.
- **Integrated deductible.** An integrated deductible may be satisfied not only by payments made by the insured but also by benefits paid by the basic plan. However, the amount of the integrated deductible is fairly high. As an example, let us suppose that an insured's basic policy pays $700 for anesthesiology services, and his supplemental major medical policy pays all additional expenses, with a $1,000 integrated deductible. If the insured is charged $1,500 for anesthesiology, the basic plan will pay the first $700, the insured will pay the difference between that amount and the $1,000 integrated deductible, or $300, and the supplemental plan will pay the remaining $500. On the other hand, if the basic plan's maximum benefit for anesthesiology was $1,200 and the supplemental plan's integrated deductible for this service was $1,000, the insured would not have to pay a deductible.

The integrated deductible is less common than the corridor deductible.

A deductible can apply to an entire family. The amount of a **family deductible** is set at two, two-and-a-half, or three times the standard deductible, but it can be satisfied by expenses incurred by any member of the family, and once it is satisfied, it is satisfied for all family members.

Coinsurance

Coinsurance is the arrangement by which the insurer and the insured each pay a percentage of covered losses after the deductible is met. For every dollar of covered expenses incurred after the deductible, the insurer typically pays 80 cents and the insured pays 20 cents. Many plans apply a dollar limit (for example, $1,000) to the coinsurance to be borne by the insured during any one calendar year. The purpose of coinsurance is to discourage the insured from using medical services unnecessarily by having her pay a portion of the expense of any service.

Overall Maximums

Many major medical policies set an overall maximum benefit, the maximum amount of money that the insurer has the obligation to pay. This maximum may be lifetime (all cause) or per cause. It is normally very high (for example, $1,000,000, $2,000,000, or even as high as $5,000,000).

Summary

All types of **medical expense insurance** provide benefits (reimbursement) for medical expenses incurred by the insured.

Hospital-surgical insurance (basic medical expense insurance) pays specified benefits for specified expenses. These benefits are somewhat limited compared to major medical coverage, but the insurer pays them without requiring the insured to contribute. The total cost to the insured will be that of any expense that the policy does not cover.

Major medical insurance usually covers more expenses and pays greater benefits for those it covers, but requires the insured to contribute by paying a deductible and coinsurance. The total cost to the insured is usually a deductible plus coinsurance (normally 20 percent) for expenses in excess of the deductible. In theory, the insured may have to pay expenses not covered by the policy, but this is much rarer than with hospital-surgical insurance, as coverage is broad and overall maximums very high.

Supplemental major medical provides this kind of coverage as a supplement to a hospital-surgical policy; **comprehensive major medical** provides in one policy the coverage of a hospital-surgical policy and a supplemental major medical policy.

This topic is covered in greater detail in the AHIP book *Medical Expense Insurance.*

4 SUPPLEMENTAL COVERAGES

- *Dental Insurance*
- *Prescription Drug Insurance*
- *Vision Care Insurance*
- *Hospital Indemnity Insurance*
- *Critical Illness Insurance*
- *Specified Disease Insurance*

- *Accidental Death and Dismemberment Insurance (AD&D)*
- *Travel Accident Insurance*
- *Accident Medical Expense Insurance*
- *Medicare Supplement Insurance*

Introduction

Supplemental coverages supplement other coverages; that is, they pay benefits that other broader coverages do not. Usually, they serve to:

- reimburse for the portion of expenses that a medical expense policy requires the insured to pay, such as deductibles and coinsurance;
- pay benefits for the kinds of expenses that a medical expense policy may exclude, such as dental, prescription drug, and vision expenses; and
- cover the nonmedical expenses that often result from a major illness, such as child care and travel and lodging for family members.

Dental Insurance

Dental insurance provides reimbursement for the expense of dental services and supplies, which are often excluded from medical expense plans.

TABLE 4.1

Nonscheduled Dental Expense Plan

Calendar Year Maximum—$1,000   Calendar Year Deductible—$50
Preventive and Diagnostic Services—100% reimbursement (no deductible)
Diagnostic: Oral exams, tests and lab exams
Preventive: Prophylaxis, fluoride treatments, space maintainers

Basic Services—80% reimbursement (20% payable by insured)
Radiographs, basic restoration (amalgam, silicate, acrylic), endodontics, periodontics, prosthodontics (maintenance), oral surgery, anesthesia

Major Services—60% reimbursement (40% payable by insured)
Major restoration (gold foil, gold inlays, porcelain, crowns), prosthodontics (installation)

Orthodontics—50% reimbursement (50% payable by the insured). Lifetime Maximum Amount—$3,000.

How Dental Plans Differ

- **Integrated vs. nonintegrated plans.** A dental plan may be integrated into a medical expense policy, or it may be an entirely separate policy (nonintegrated or stand-alone).
- **Scheduled vs. nonscheduled (usual and customary) reimbursement.** A dental plan may reimburse for dental services based on a schedule or based on the usual and customary charges for services. A dental schedule, like a surgical schedule, specifies amounts for given services and reimburses up to that amount. These amounts may vary with geography to reflect the level of charges in different areas of the country. Generally, integrated plans reimburse on a nonscheduled basis, while nonintegrated plans may reimburse on either basis.

Classification of Dental Services

Most plans divide dental services into classes and use different deductibles, coinsurance, and maximum benefits for each class. The usual classes are:

- diagnostic
- preventive
- restorative (including fillings, inlays, and crowns)
- prosthodontics (installment and maintenance of bridgework)
- oral surgery
- periodontics or endodontics (treatment of gums)
- orthodontics (straightening treatment)

FIGURE 4.1

Distribution of Charges for Dental Services, 1997

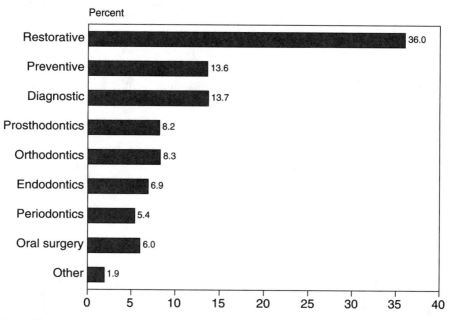

Source: Mutual of Omaha, Current Trends, 1998.

Deductibles, Coinsurance, and Maximum Benefits

- **Deductibles.** Like medical expense plans, most dental plans have a deductible that must be satisfied by each individual during each calendar year. In most integrated plans there is a single deductible for both dental and medical expenses. To encourage preventive care, the deductible is usually not applied to preventive and diagnostic services.
- **Coinsurance.** Most dental plans also have coinsurance. Percentages of coinsurance may be different for different classes of services and usually range from 20 percent to 50 percent. The percentage of coinsurance is usually greater for major procedures than for basic procedures.
- **Maximum benefit.** Some nonintegrated dental plans have a calendar year or policy year maximum on benefits. Some have a lifetime maximum for orthodontic benefits, and some also have a lifetime maximum on periodontal care.

Limitations, Exclusions, and Options

- The frequency of some services may be limited. For example, typically no more than two dental cleanings and one fluoride treatment may be covered in any 12 consecutive months. Bridgework or dentures may not be replaced within a five-year period except under specific circumstances.
- Cosmetic and experimental services are excluded.
- Replacement of teeth missing prior to the effective date of the dental plan may be excluded entirely or covered at a reduced reimbursement rate.
- Orthodontic services are expensive, and including them in a policy can significantly increase premiums. Therefore, they are usually an option that the insured may choose and pay for.

Prescription Drug Insurance

Prescription drug insurance covers drugs and medicines prescribed by a physician. Most plans are offered through an employer on a group basis.

Copayments

Up to this point we have discussed two arrangements by which the insured shares health care costs: the deductible and coinsurance. Prescription drug plans typically use another arrangement, the copayment. A copayment is a flat dollar amount that the insured pays each time a certain kind of service is received. The copayment is not a percentage of the total cost, like coinsurance, but rather is always the same dollar amount even though the total cost of the service may vary. In the case of prescription drug plans, for example, the insured might pay $10 for any prescription, regardless of the actual cost of the prescription. Prescription plan copayments typically range from $5 to $15 and can be as high as $50. The copayment for generic drugs is usually lower.

Reimbursement Plans and Service Plans

There are two types of prescription drug plans: reimbursement and service.

- In **reimbursement plans,** the insured pays a pharmacist for prescribed drugs, the pharmacist completes a claim form, the insured submits the form to the insurer, and the insurer reimburses the insured. Reimbursement is based on usual and customary charges.
- In **service plans,** the insured obtains prescription drugs from a pharmacist who participates in the plan. The insured does not pay the pharmacist or pays only a copayment. The insurer then reimburses the pharmacist.

Service plans require extensive networks of participating pharmacies and involve a large number of small claims. Third-party administrators generally manage the plans for insurance companies because their high volume of business allows them to minimize administrative costs and negotiate discounts with participating pharmacies.

Service plans include mail-order prescription drug programs. These plans serve those who use maintenance medication and find it convenient to order 60- or 90-day supplies.

Exclusions and Limitations

- Drugs that are dispensed while the individual is confined in a hospital or extended care facility are usually excluded, as they are normally covered by regular medical expense insurance.
- Prescriptions are usually limited to a specified number of days' supply of a drug. The limit is typically a 30-day supply for drugs obtained from a regular pharmacy and a 90-day supply for drugs obtained from a mail-order pharmacy.
- Devices of any type, such as hypodermic needles or syringes, and bandages, are usually excluded.
- Sexual dysfunction drugs, beauty aids or cosmetics, dietary supplements, immunization agents, sera, and blood or blood plasma are usually excluded.
- Contraceptive drugs or medicines are normally excluded, but may be covered at the policyholder's request for an additional premium.

Vision Care Insurance

Vision care insurance provides benefits for routine preventive and corrective vision care. This coverage is usually offered on a group basis as a complement to other group coverages.

Covered Expenses

Vision care insurance normally provides reimbursement for:

- eye examinations (including refraction);
- single vision, bifocal, and trifocal lenses;
- contact lenses;
- other aids for subnormal vision (such as lenticular lenses); and
- frames (with limitations, see below).

Under most vision care programs, the services covered require the authorization of an ophthalmologist or optometrist.

Reimbursement

Vision plans reimburse insureds in one of three ways:

- reimbursement for all expenses up to a flat dollar maximum per individual per calendar year;
- reimbursement based on usual and customary charges; or
- reimbursement based on a specified schedule.

Limitations and Exclusions

- Policies often limit coverage to one examination and one pair of lenses in any 12 consecutive months and one pair of frames every two years.
- Expenses for frames are usually limited to a certain amount. This amount covers average frames; those who choose luxury frames must pay the added cost. Other nonessential items such as sunglasses, tinted lenses, and safety glasses are generally excluded, as is duplication due to breakage or loss.
- Medical or surgical treatment is commonly excluded, as this is covered by medical expense plans.

Hospital Indemnity Insurance

Hospital indemnity coverage pays a flat dollar amount for each day, week, or month the insured is confined in a hospital. Hospital indemnity benefits are not based on actual expenses incurred by the insured and are paid in addition to and regardless of any other benefits the insured may receive. The purpose of this coverage is to provide money for the insured to pay for:

- out-of-pocket payments required by other coverages, such as deductibles, coinsurance, copayments, and payments for expenses that exceed overall maximums;
- medical expenses not covered by other insurance policies, such as experimental treatments, additional medical opinions, additional prescription drugs, rehabilitation services, and home health care; and
- incidental expenses incurred during the illness, such as child care, transportation, home or auto modification, housekeeping, and lost income of both the patient and family members who must take time off work.

The amount of benefits typically ranges from $100 to $400 per day. Benefits are paid from the first day of hospital confinement and are paid for either a sickness or injury. A maximum benefit period is set, generally three, six, or twelve months. This type of protection usually is offered as an optional supplement to group or individual medical expense insurance.

Critical Illness Insurance

Critical illness insurance is similar in many ways to hospital indemnity insurance. Like hospital indemnity benefits, critical illness benefits:

- are not based on actual expenses;
- are paid in addition to and regardless of any other benefits the insured may receive; and
- are intended to provide money for the insured to pay for out-of-pocket payments, medical expenses not paid by other coverage, and incidental expenses.

The difference between the two coverages is that while the amount paid by hospital indemnity insurance is based on the amount of time the insured spends in the hospital, critical illness insurance pays a lump sum. This lump sum is paid if the insured suffers from one of the serious illnesses or injuries specified in the policy. Typically covered are heart attack, angioplasty, heart bypass, major organ transplant, stroke, kidney failure, paralysis, cancer, Alzheimer's disease, multiple sclerosis, and the loss of sight, limb, hearing, or speech.

The amount of the lump sum paid by a policy varies according to the seriousness of the illness or injury. Different policies have higher or lower benefit levels (with maximums ranging from $10,000 to $2,000,000) and charge higher or lower premiums. The lump sum payment is usually made following a waiting period of 30 days after the confirmed diagnosis of a covered illness or accident.

Critical illness insurance is available to persons age 18 through 64. Coverage terminates after the lump sum payment has been made or the insured reaches termination age (usually 65). Policies are available as stand-alone individual coverage, employer group coverage, or riders to existing life insurance policies.

Specified Disease Insurance

Specified disease insurance pays benefits in the event the insured suffers from one stipulated disease. Benefits are paid for this disease only, not for any other disease or any accident. The most common type of specified disease policy is cancer insurance, and it accounts for the largest portion of the market.

Like hospital indemnity insurance and critical illness insurance, specified disease insurance usually pays benefits in addition to those received from other insurance policies and so serves to provide the insured with money to pay for expenses not covered by his other insurance—out-of-pocket payments, noncovered medical expenses, and incidental costs. Incidental costs may be large for cancer patients and their families, who may incur transportation, food, and lodging expenses when they travel to other cities for specialized care.

Some specified disease policies pay flat dollar amounts like hospital indemnity insurance, but more often they work like major medical policies, paying benefits for such items as cancer screening tests, daily room and board, physician visits, nursing, and drugs and medicines. Maximum benefits of $50,000 to $150,000 are common.

Accidental Death and Dismemberment Insurance (AD&D)

Accidental death and dismemberment insurance pays benefits when the insured dies, loses the sight of one or both eyes, or loses a hand or a foot directly as a result of an accidental bodily injury. It is usually offered on a group basis.

Description of Benefits

An accidental death and dismemberment policy establishes an amount known as the **principal sum**. Benefits are all or part of this amount. Typical benefits are as follows:

- For loss of life, the full principal sum is paid (to the insured's designated beneficiary).
- For severance of a hand or foot at or above the wrist or ankle, or for irrecoverable loss of sight of one eye, one-half the principal sum is paid.
- For more than one loss of hand, foot, or eye from the same accident, the full principal sum is paid. However, the benefit for any one accident never exceeds the principal sum, even if there are more than two losses.

Limitations and Exclusions

Benefits are not payable for any loss that results directly or indirectly, wholly or partly, from any of the following:

- disease or bodily or mental infirmity or their medical or surgical treatment (since AD&D is an *accident* coverage);
- ptomaine or bacterial infection, except infections occurring through an accidental cut or wound;
- suicide or an intentionally self-inflicted injury;
- war or any act of war; or
- drug use, unless drugs are taken as prescribed by a physician.

How AD&D Plans Differ

- **Nonoccupational vs. 24-hour.** All AD&D policies are either nonoccupational or 24-hour. Nonoccupational policies do not cover accidents resulting from the insured's employment. Twenty-four hour policies cover accidents occurring at any time, on or off the job.
- **Group life supplement vs. voluntary.** An AD&D policy may be sold as a nonoptional supplement to an employer's group life insurance. Or it may be sold on a voluntary basis. Voluntary AD&D is also group insurance, and employees usually pay premiums through payroll deductions, but each employee may choose whether to receive and pay for the coverage.

The principal sum of a group life supplement AD&D policy is usually the same as the benefit of the group life insurance. Although the life insurance policy may continue after the retirement of the insured, the AD&D supplement usually does not.

Business Trip AD&D

This coverage, a form of travel accident insurance (see below), is designed for employers who provide supplementary accident protection for their employees when they travel on company business. The cost of this coverage usually is paid entirely by the employer.

Generally, three types of business trip accident plans are offered:

- **Comprehensive (or all risk) plans** provide 24-hour protection for the employee's entire trip, from the time the employee leaves her home or place of business until she returns.
- **Common carrier plans** cover only accidents involving common carriers (public conveyances licensed and used for the transportation of passengers).
- **All conveyance plans** cover accidents involving any sort of conveyance, including personal or company-owned vehicles.

Dependents AD&D

AD&D plans for employees may also cover their dependents. Dependent AD&D is always 24-hour, regardless of what coverage is provided for employees. Eligible dependents include the employee's spouse and unmarried children, up to a specified age.

Travel Accident Insurance

Travel accident insurance provides benefits in case of accidental death or dismemberment while the insured is a passenger on a common carrier such as an airplane. The protection is for a single trip, usually on a round-trip basis. Policies are purchased primarily at vending machines in airports, bus terminals, and railroad stations, and from representatives of insurers at many of the larger airports. They are also sold at travel agencies, where they may be purchased as an option or prepackaged into the traveler's tour plan. Various credit card companies also provide travel accident insurance as an additional benefit.

Even though the coverage provided is very similar to that of AD&D, travel accident insurance is usually classified as a different type of insurance because of the different methods used to sell it. These sales methods make this very limited type of coverage available at low cost.

Accident Medical Expense Insurance

Accident medical expense insurance reimburses for care needed because of an accidental injury. Benefits are not paid for any disease. Benefits include treatment by a physician, hospital care, nursing care, and X-ray and laboratory work. This coverage usually supplements regular medical expense insurance.

Generally, the coverage applies only if the expenses are incurred within a specified time (usually three or six months) from the date of the accident. Benefits are subject to an overall maximum benefit for any one accident. Some plans have small deductibles (for example, $25); others do not. (That is, they provide first-dollar coverage.)

Medicare Supplement Insurance

Medicare supplement insurance reimburses for expenses not covered by the federal government's Medicare program. Medicare pays for health care for people age 65 and over. However, Medicare does have deductibles and coinsurance amounts, and there is no limit to the amount that a beneficiary of the program may have to pay out of her own pocket. Therefore, senior citizens may incur considerable expense as a result of long-term hospitalization or prolonged illness.

To understand Medicare supplement insurance, we must first understand the Medicare program. Medicare benefits are divided into Part A and Part B.

Medicare Part A Benefits

Medicare Part A is provided automatically to persons age 65 and older who are eligible for Social Security retirement benefits. It is financed by earnings deductions paid by employers and employees.

Medicare Part A pays benefits for hospitalization, skilled nursing facilities, home health services, hospice care, and blood. Hospitalization benefits and out-of-pocket expenses include:

- **The first 60 days.** A Medicare beneficiary who is hospitalized must pay an initial deductible, after which Medicare pays 100 percent of the hospital charges for the first 60 days of confinement.
- **The 61st to the 90th day.** During this period, the beneficiary must pay a copayment for each day of hospital confinement.
- **After the 90th day.** In general, after 90 days the beneficiary is responsible for all expenses. There is one exception—each beneficiary has a lifetime benefit of up to 60 additional days that are covered on the same basis as the period from the 61st through the 90th day (that is, the beneficiary pays a copayment and Medicare pays the rest). The beneficiary can use these 60 days during one period of hospitalization or during several different periods, but once he has used a total of 60 days, the benefit ends.

Other Medicare Part A benefits are as follows:

- Part A pays for **service in an approved skilled nursing facility** for up to 100 days per spell of illness. The beneficiary must first spend at least three days in a hospital. Then, Medicare pays all costs of the first 20 days of the nursing home stay. For days 21 through 100, the beneficiary pays a daily copayment.
- **Home health services** are provided for up to 21 days (intermittent or consecutive) per spell of illness.
- **Hospice benefits** for terminally ill patients are paid for a lifetime limit of 210 days.
- All **blood** the beneficiary needs, after a deductible of the first three pints, also is covered.

Medicare Part B Benefits

Medicare Part B, supplementary medical insurance, is a voluntary program. Beneficiaries must pay a portion of the premiums. However, this portion is only 25 percent; the government pays the other 75 percent.

TABLE 4.2

Standardized Medicare Supplement Policies

Benefits	"Core" A	B	C	D	E	F	G	H	I	J
CORE benefits										
Part A hospital (Days 61–90)	X	X	X	X	X	X	X	X	X	X
Lifetime reserve (Days 91–150)	X	X	X	X	X	X	X	X	X	X
365 Lifetime hospital (Days at 100%)	X	X	X	X	X	X	X	X	X	X
Part A and Part B blood	X	X	X	X	X	X	X	X	X	X
Part B coinsurance–20%	X	X	X	X	X	X	X	X	X	X
Additional benefits										
Skilled nursing facility (Days 21–100)			X	X	X	X	X	X	X	X
Part A deductible		X	X	X	X	X	X	X	X	X
Part B deductible			X			X				X
Part B excess charges						100%	80%		100%	100%
Foreign travel			X	X	X	X	X	X	X	X
At-home recovery				X			X		X	X
Preventive medical care					X					X
Prescription drugs								Basic	Basic	Extended

Part B provides benefits such as physicians' treatments, surgical procedures, hospital outpatient services, and medical supplies. It does not pay for prescription drugs. Medicare bases its payment on what it deems reasonable for the geographic area in which the service was provided. The beneficiary pays a calendar year deductible plus 20 percent coinsurance. It should also be noted that Medicare Part B does not cover all possible expenses, so the beneficiary may be responsible for these as well.

Medicare Supplement Policies

As of November 1991 the federal government requires all Medicare supplement policies to be standardized into ten plans labeled A through J. Insurance companies marketing these plans must offer Plan A, which is generally referred to as the core plan. They may offer any or all of the other nine plans. (See Table 4.2.)

Summary

There are many different health insurance coverages that serve to supplement medical expense insurance. These coverages both pay for medical services not covered by other policies and reimburse the insured for his share of expenses under other policies (such as deductibles and coinsurance). Supplemental coverages can be studied in more detail in AHIP's book *Supplemental Health Insurance*.

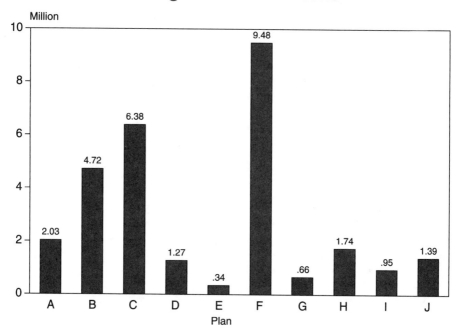

FIGURE 4.2

Distribution of MedSupp (Medigap) Policies Among 29 Million Persons

Source: Physician Payment Review Commission, 1996 Annual Report to Congress.

5 DISABILITY INCOME COVERAGE AND LONG-TERM CARE COVERAGE

- *Types of Disability Income Insurance*
- *Disability Benefit Provisions*
- *Qualifications for Disability Benefits*
- *Total Disability, Residual Disability, and Earned Income*
- *Additional Disability Income Coverages*
- *Functional Capacity*
- *Long-Term Care Benefits, Limitations, and Exclusions*

Introduction

Medical expense insurance pays most of the costs of hospital and medical care. Supplemental coverages help pay the remaining costs as well as other health-related expenses not covered by medical expense insurance, such as dental care or prescription drugs. But we also face the possibility of needing financial help over a long period of time. For example, a person may find herself unable to work and earn a living for months or years because of an illness or injury. Or a person may become unable to fully take care of herself and may need care in a nursing facility or require home nursing services on an indefinite basis. Disability income insurance and long-term care insurance protect against these situations.

Disability Income Insurance

Disability income insurance protects the insured against loss of income in the event he is unable to work due to an illness or injury. Although the term disability income insurance is becoming increasingly accepted, a number of synonyms such as "income protection insurance" and "loss of time insurance" are still used.

Types of Coverage

Disability income insurance is offered on both an individual and group basis. Group insurance is often referred to as long-term disability (LTD) insurance, not to be confused with long-term care insurance. The benefits provided by group and individual coverages are similar.

In addition, some policies cover only disability caused by accidental injury, while others cover both illness and injury. Benefits provided under the two approaches are otherwise similar in all respects.

Benefit Provisions

Each disability income policy has three provisions, agreed upon by insurer and insured, that together determine what benefits are payable.

Monthly or weekly indemnity. The monthly or weekly indemnity is the amount paid to the insured on a monthly or weekly basis during total disability. This amount is not determined by the insured's actual loss of income. Rather, the insured and the insurer agree in advance to an amount. The insured will want an amount that provides her with enough income to live on, but must also keep in mind that the higher the indemnity, the higher the premiums she will pay. From the insurer's point of view, the higher the indemnity, the more it earns in premiums, but the insurer does not want the amount to be so high that the insured has a financial incentive to become or remain disabled. Therefore, the insurer limits the indemnity amount so that it is not greater than or nearly equal to the insured's normal income. Thus, although the insured's income does not directly determine the amount of the indemnity, it is taken into account in setting the amount.

Most insurers set maximum indemnity amounts for given income levels. Sometimes these maximums are expressed as a percentage of the insured's income, ranging from 30 percent (for very high incomes) to 80 percent (for low incomes). The percentages for low-income insureds are higher because they need a higher portion of their regular income to maintain a reasonable lifestyle.

In addition, most insurers have a maximum indemnity amount regardless of income. This maximum varies primarily according to the occupation of the insured. Maximum monthly indemnities are typically between $10,000 and $15,000, but they can be higher for persons under the age of 50 in the most low-risk occupations.

Monthly indemnity amounts can be as small as $100. However, many insurers will not sell disability income coverage to persons with incomes below a certain level (such as $18,000). This is because people with limited incomes find it difficult to pay premiums and often let their policies lapse. Not all insurers have minimum income requirements.

Elimination period. The elimination period (also called the benefit waiting period) is the length of time at the beginning of a period of disability for which no benefits are payable. The most common elimination periods are 30, 60, 90, and 180 days. Elimination periods serve the same function for disability insurance that deductibles serve for medical expense coverage—they help reduce the insurer's administrative costs by eliminating many small claims. This helps keep premiums more affordable for the insureds.

Maximum benefit period. The maximum benefit period (also called the indemnity limit) is the maximum length of time for which benefits are payable during any one period of disability. The most commonly offered maximum benefit periods are one year, two years, five years, and to age 65.

Qualifications for Benefits

To be eligible to receive benefits, the insured must be under a physician's care, and the disability must be due to a cause covered by the policy. Some causes are subject to exclusions and limitations, as with medical expense insurance. These include preexisting conditions, pregnancy, self-inflicted injuries or attempted suicide, active military duty, and war.

Two benefit situations are recognized: **total disability** and **residual disability**. Total disability means the complete loss of the ability to earn a living; residual disability (or permanent partial disability) refers to reduced earning ability. In this case the insured is able to work but unable to perform some of his normal job duties or unable to work full time. Very often the insured has been totally disabled and no longer is, but suffers a continuing impairment or illness (hence "residual").

Qualifications for total disability. Total disability may be defined in two ways:

- **Own-occupation definition.** The insured is considered totally disabled if she is unable to engage in her own normal occupation.
- **Any-occupation definition.** The insured is considered totally disabled only if she is unable to engage in any gainful occupation for which she is reasonably suited by education, training, or experience.

A group disability income policy usually uses both definitions. During an initial period of disability (such as the first two or three years), the own-occupation definition applies. After the initial period the any-occupation definition applies. In the individual field, there have traditionally been two types of policies: those that use only the own-occupation definition no matter how long the insured is disabled, and less expensive policies that use only the any-occupation definition. However, many individual policies now follow the two-period approach used in group insurance. This approach has become more widespread because it is a compromise that offers some of the advantages of each of the two traditional policy types. It is less expensive than a strict own-occupation policy, but it provides a period of adjustment during which the own-occupation definition applies, which a strict any-occupation policy does not. This adjustment period gives an insured who will not be able to continue in her previous occupation the opportunity to get additional training or education.

Qualifications for residual disability. In most cases, residual disability benefits are payable if the insured meets all of these conditions:

- He has a continuing disability but is able to work full- or part-time in his regular occupation or any other occupation.
- He earns a current income that is at least 20 percent (25 percent in some policies) less than prior monthly earned income.
- He continues to be under the care of a physician.

Residual Disability Benefits

As stated above, the monthly or weekly indemnity amount is not based on the insured's actual loss of income but rather is agreed to in advance by the insured and the insurer. This is the amount paid for total disability. However, in the case of residual disability, the amount of benefits is based on the amount the insured's income has been reduced by the disability. To determine the amount of income reduction, the insured's earned income during residual disability is compared with his earned income before the disability. The amount of benefits will be a portion of income reduction—as with total disability, the insurer does not want benefits to exceed or nearly equal the insured's normal income, as this would give her an incentive to remain on disability.

Earned income is defined (for both the pre-disability and the disabled periods) as income received from salary, wages, fees, commissions, or other remuneration earned by the insured for services performed. Earned income is determined before deduction of federal or state taxes. If the insured is self-employed, earned income means gross income less normal and customary business expenses. Insurers normally base pre-disability income on the insured's average income during a 12- or 24-month period before the disability occurred.

Additional Coverages

Some disability income policies may have additional coverages. Some of these are optional and require an increased premium.

- **Short-term monthly indemnity.** This coverage pays a certain amount every month in addition to the regular monthly payments during the first few months of total disability. This added payment is usually limited to five or six months, although some insurers pay up to one year. Its purpose is to provide additional income in the months before the insured becomes eligible for Social Security disability benefits.

- **Social insurance substitute (SIS).** This coverage provides additional monthly disability benefits during periods when the insured is not receiving benefits from government social insurance programs (such as Social Security disability or retirement benefits, workers' compensation, state no-fault insurance, and various other state disability programs). Payments are generally up to $1,000 per month. If and when the insured qualifies for a government social insurance program, the monthly benefits provided by the SIS are terminated or reduced by the amount of the government benefit.
- **Future increase option (guaranteed insurability option).** Disability income insurance is intended to provide the disabled with an income similar to what he earned while working. His earned income may of course increase over the years, and the indemnity amount initially agreed upon may become inadequate to compensate for the possible loss of this increased income. The future increase option gives the insured the right to increase this amount at specified future option dates. Because the insured has this right regardless of medical insurability, this coverage is also known as the "Guaranteed Insurability Option." The increase allowed is both limited to certain stipulated amounts and based on the income growth of the insured.
- **Return-of-premium option.** This option gives the insured the right to get back a percentage (usually between 50 and 80 percent) of the total premium after specified periods of time (for example, every five or ten years) if she does not become disabled. The insured must pay an extra premium for this option.
- **Cost-of-living adjustment (COLA).** Under this provision, benefit payments are increased to compensate for the effects of inflation during a lengthy period of disability.

Business-Oriented Disability Coverages

The prolonged disability of a business owner can result in the economic death of the business. Business-oriented disability coverages were developed to protect against this risk.

Overhead expense insurance. Small businesses and professional practices often depend on the activities of one or two people to generate the income needed to meet business expenses. Overhead expense insurance compensates the insured for business expenses incurred during total disability. Overhead expense insurance does not pay a monthly benefit like other varieties of disability insurance—it reimburses for actual expenses.

Overhead expenses are defined as the usual and necessary expenses of the operation of a business or professional practice. Expenses usually covered are monthly rent, interest on mortgage payments, employee salaries, utilities, postage, business laundry, and association or trade dues and subscriptions. Expenses not usually covered are the insured's salary, compensation of any person hired to perform the insured's duties, purchase of goods and merchandise, payment on the principal of any indebtedness, and any expenses not regularly and customarily incurred before the disability.

Key-employee disability income insurance. Like overhead expense insurance, key-employee disability income insurance protects a business from the loss of earnings that can occur when an important employee is disabled, and benefits are paid to the business, not the disabled employee. However, unlike in overhead expense insurance, benefits are a monthly amount, not the amount of actual expenses. Insurers usually sell this coverage only to small businesses.

Disability buyout insurance (business interest insurance). This coverage provides the funds for the purchase of the business interest of a partner or stockholder who becomes disabled. The partners or stockholders prepare a formal buy/sell agreement in advance. This agreement provides that if one of them becomes disabled for a certain length of time, generally two years, the disabled person is obliged to sell his interest and the other partners or stockholders are obliged to buy it. The agreement specifies the price (or a formula calculating the price) at which the business interest will be sold.

Recent Developments in Disability Income Insurance

The disability income insurance field has undergone major change since the late 1980s. **Morbidity** (the frequency and severity of illnesses and accidents) among insureds has increased, resulting in an increase in claims and a rise in premium rates (necessary to cover the greater cost of claims). Consequently, disability income insurance has become both less profitable to insurers and less affordable to consumers. In response, a number of insurers have stopped offering this coverage, and those that still do have had to make drastic changes to make it profitable and affordable again. Changes have been in pricing, coverage provisions and features, underwriting requirements and standards, administration of claims, and the payment of sales commissions.

Long-Term Care Insurance

Long-term care insurance provides benefits when an insured suffers a loss of functional capacity and so needs the assistance of another person to perform the necessary activities of life. Such assistance is provided in a nursing home or by home nursing care providers.

Functional Capacity

Loss of functional capacity is usually defined as the need for assistance to perform some or all of the following functions, known as **activities of daily living (ADLs):**

- bathing—getting into and out of a shower or tub;
- dressing—putting on and taking off all necessary items of clothing;
- transferring—moving between the bed and a chair or the bed and a wheelchair;
- toileting—getting to and from the toilet, getting on and off the toilet, and associated personal hygiene;
- eating—getting food into the body; and
- continence—voluntary control over bowel or bladder.

The loss of functional capacity may have either physical or cognitive causes. It may result from an injury or a disease (including an organic brain disease), but it is often simply a result of aging.

Benefits

Long-term care plans usually pay between $50 and $300 for each day of confinement in a nursing care facility and between $20 and $150 for each day of home health care.

- **Elimination period.** Some policies have an elimination period provision, under which benefits are payable only after a specified time. This is usually a certain number of consecutive days (often 90) during which the insured suffers loss of functional capacity. Some insurers offer an option with no elimination period. Prior hospitalization or nursing home confinement is not required for the insured to begin receiving benefits.
- **Benefit period.** The period during which the insured is receiving benefits is the benefit period. The benefit period begins on the first day following the end of the elimination period. If the insured regains functional capacity for an extended period, the benefit period ends. Generally, the benefit period ends after the insured has regained functional capacity for 60 days in a row.

An insured may regain functional capacity and then lose it again. In this case, some policies require a separate elimination period for each benefit period. Other policies provide that the elimination period must be satisfied only once per lifetime rather than once per benefit period.

When an insured is receiving benefit payments, he is not required to pay premiums. Premium payments start again on the first premium due date following the end of a benefit period.

Requirements for Personnel and Facilities

The personnel and facilities that provide services to the insured must meet certain requirements. A nursing facility must be licensed or legally qualified to provide nursing care or assistance in performing activities of daily living (ADLs). Home health care must be provided through a home health agency and performed by a registered nurse, licensed practical nurse, vocational nurse, home health aide, licensed certified or registered occupational therapist, speech therapist, or physical therapist. Home health care must be performed in the insured's own home, another private home, a facility for the retired or aged, or a licensed or legally qualified adult day care center operating for the purpose of providing nursing, medical, and health-related social services.

Limitations and Exclusions

If the insured loses functional capacity as a result of a preexisting condition, benefits are not provided unless the loss of capacity occurs more than six (sometimes 12) months after the effective date of the policy.

A loss of functional capacity resulting from the following is also generally excluded:

- mental, nervous, or emotional disorders (although organic brain diseases such as Alzheimer's disease are usually covered);
- alcoholism or drug addiction; and
- self-inflicted injuries or attempted suicide.

In addition, benefits are not paid for the following expenses:

- expenses incurred any day the insured is confined in a hospital;
- nursing care or home health care expenses covered under other types of health insurance;
- expenses for which reimbursement is available under a government program; or
- expenses for care received outside the United States.

Portability

When long-term care insurance is purchased through an employer-sponsored plan, employees who leave that employer generally may continue coverage for themselves, spouses, and others. In this case, premiums are paid by the individual directly to the insurer.

Inflation Protection

People expect that if they actually need nursing home care or home nursing services, it will be far in the future, in their old age. Consequently, inflation is a concern. Some policies address this concern by giving the insured the right to

FIGURE 5.1

Individual and Group Association Long-Term Care Policies Sold, 1987–1996

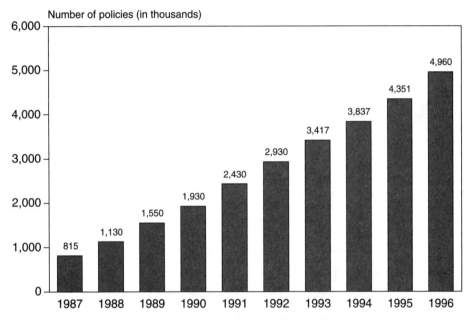

Number of policies (in thousands)

Source: Health Insurance Association of America, Long-Term Care Survey, 1998.

purchase periodic increases in benefits. These increases are often based on changes in the consumer price index (CPI). The premium paid by the insured will also be increased to reflect both the additional amount of benefits and the age of the insured when the additional benefits are purchased.

Other policies offer an alternative arrangement. They guarantee an annual increase (for example, 5 percent) in benefits. Such policies charge a higher premium, but this premium will not be changed for the life of the policy.

Current Trends in Long-Term Care Insurance

Long-term care insurance has tremendous market potential. There has been steady growth in this coverage in recent years, and this growth is expected to continue. (See Figure 5.1.)

Summary

We need health insurance protection not only to pay the costs of health care, but also for income protection so that we will not lose our savings or become destitute due to an inability to work. Disability income insurance provides this protection. In addition, we all face the possibility of needing long-term living assistance such as nursing home care or in-home nursing care. Long-term care coverage meets this need. As advances in medical science help us live longer, the likelihood increases that each of us will at some point need long-term care coverage. More can be learned about both of these coverages in other AHIP books listed in the back of this book.

6 FLEXIBLE BENEFIT PLANS

- *Advantages of Flexible Benefit Plans*
- *Designing a Flexible Benefit Plan*
- *Issues Related to Flexible Benefit Plans*

Introduction

Historically, employers who provided their employees with group insurance chose one policy for each type of coverage (life, medical expense, disability, etc.), and all employees were provided with the same policies. This has changed during the past two decades with the implementation of flexible benefit plans, also called cafeteria plans. These are arrangements whereby employers can offer their employees a selection of insurance options. The individual employee can choose whether or not she wants a particular coverage (for example, whether or not she wants long-term care insurance). She can also usually choose between different plans of the same type (for example, two or three medical expense plans).

Often, the employer provides each employee with an amount of credits that she can apply to whatever combination of benefits she chooses. If the employee wants more benefits than are covered by the credits, she may pay for the additional benefits by means of a pretax salary deduction.

Advantages of Flexible Benefit Plans

Flexible benefit plans have two primary advantages: employee satisfaction and cost control.

Employee Satisfaction

Every employee has different insurance needs, depending on his family status, sex, age, lifestyle, health status, and income. A flexible benefit plan allows each employee to make the most of employer benefit dollars and get the benefits he values most. As the benefits package is usually a significant portion of an employee's total compensation, the design of the package can be a significant element in overall employee satisfaction and an important factor in the decision of a prospective employee to accept a job. Today, just as they expect to have choices in many other areas of life, most people expect the choice of flexible benefit plans, and many employers see them as state-of-the-art benefit packages consistent with the image of a progressive and innovative company.

Cost Control

Flexible benefit plans allow employers to limit health insurance cost increases by encouraging employees to use managed care plans. And because health care is such a large and growing part of an employer's total payroll costs, this use of flexible benefit plans for cost control is of major importance.

Flexible benefit plans encourage the use of managed care by giving employees financial incentives to choose it. Typically, a traditional plan and a managed care plan are offered, and since employee contributions to premiums reflect the actual cost of each plan, premiums are considerably lower for the managed care plan. This cost differential also increases the awareness of all employees of the relative cost and efficiency of the different kinds of plans.

Designing a Flexible Benefit Plan

There are three basic flexible benefit plan designs: modular, core-plus, and full flexible.

Modular Format

In this format, employees choose among three or four benefit packages. Each package is designed to meet the needs of a certain broad type of employee (for example, young singles, families, etc.). (See Table 6.1.)

TABLE 6.1

Modular Format Flexible Benefit Plan

Benefits	Option 1 package	Option 2 package	Option 3 package
Life insurance	2 × salary	1 × salary	3 × salary
LTD	50% of salary	50% of salary	70% of salary
Vision insurance	None	Vision plans	None
Dental insurance	Dental	No dental	Dental
Rx	Drug plan	Drug plan	None
Medical insurance	$1,000 deductible or HMO	$500 deductible or HMO	$250 deductible or HMO

TABLE 6.2

Core-Plus Format Flexible Benefit Plan

Benefits	Core (mandatory)	Optional benefits (voluntary)
Life insurance	1 × salary	1½ × salary 2 × salary 3 × salary
Dependent life insurance	None	$10,000 spouse/$5,000 child
Medical insurance	$1,000 deductible	$500 deductible $250 deductible HMO option PPO option
Dental insurance	None	$50 deductible/$1,000 maximum $75 deductible/$2,500 maximum
LTD	50% of salary	60% of salary 70% of salary
Health care reimbursement account	None	$5 to $100 monthly employee dollars
Dependent care reimbursement account	None	$50 to $400 monthly employee dollars

Core-Plus Format

The core-plus format provides a basic package of benefits usually paid for by the employer and covering all employees. A number of optional benefits can be made available, funded either through flexible credits provided by the employer, employee contributions, or a combination of the two. (See Table 6.2.)

Full-Flexible Format

The full-flexible format allows employees to choose freely from multiple options in each type of coverage independently, and permits large and varied combinations of benefits. This allows employees to customize a benefit package that meets their needs and lifestyle. (See Table 6.3.)

TABLE 6.3

Full-Flexible Format Flexible Benefit Plan

Life options	Long-term disability options
Option A—1 × salary Option B—2 × salary Option C—3 × salary	Option A—50% of salary to $5,000 Option B—60% of salary to $5,000

Medical options	Dental options

HMO coverage or comprehensive medical, $1,000,000 maximum
  Option A—HMO
  Option B—$250 deductible PPO
  Option C—$500 deductible PPO
  Option D—No participation*
 	
*Proof of coverage by another plan is usually required.
	Option A—No participation
	Option B—$1,000 maximum
	  $50 deductible
	Option C—$2,000 maximum
	  $75 deductible

Issues Related to Flexible Benefit Plans

Flexible benefit plans present challenges as well as advantages:

Planning

Under the traditional system, it is easy for the employer and the insurer to predict how many employees will have which coverages, since all employees have the same benefits. Under a flexible benefit plan, it may be hard to predict how many employees will choose which options. Many employers deal with this problem by beginning with a plan design that offers relatively few options, such as the modular format. Then they gradually introduce more choices. In this way, unpredictability is limited, as employee preferences become gradually known as more and more choice is offered.

Adverse Selection

Let us suppose that a number of people are offered a choice between a health insurance policy with greater benefits and greater premiums and another policy with fewer benefits and lower premiums. Usually, those who have more health problems (or are more likely to have problems due to age or other reasons) will choose the plan with greater benefits. Those who are young and healthy are more likely to choose the cheaper plan. As a result, the enrollees of the more comprehensive plan include a disproportionate number of the people who will actually incur expenses. This is adverse selection (also known as **anti-selection** or **selection against the insurer**), and it occurs in any situation in which people have choices, including flexible benefit plans. It is the primary disadvantage of flexible benefit plans.

Summary

Flexible benefit plans are a way to provide people with a benefit package adapted to their needs. It is also a way of giving people choices in deciding what benefits they will receive. Finally, it is a way for employers to allocate health care dollars in the most cost-effective way possible.

7 THE INSURANCE CONTRACT

- *The Basic Elements of a Contract*
- *The Contract, the Policy, and the Application*
- *Legal Principles of Health Insurance Contracts*
- *Definitions in the Insurance Contract*
- *Contract Execution*
- *Contract Renewal and Revision*
- *Emerging Trends*

Introduction

A contract is a voluntary, written, legally binding agreement between two parties (persons or other entities such as businesses or government agencies). An insurance contract is an agreement between an insurer and a policyholder by which the insurer agrees to compensate the policyholder for a loss in return for the premiums paid to the insurer. The provisions of a policy spell out all the terms and conditions of the arrangement and the rights and obligations of the parties.

The parties to an insurance contract (that is, the insurer and the policyholder) are not completely free to reach any agreement they wish. Laws and regulations govern the types of forms that must be used and stipulate that a contract must contain certain provisions (required provisions) and may contain other provisions (optional provisions). This chapter gives an overview of the most important legal principles that help to shape the health insurance contract. Subsequent chapters will discuss specific provisions and the legal requirements that govern them.

The Basic Elements of a Contract

All contracts must have these four elements to be legally binding:

- consideration
- meeting of the minds

- capacity to contract
- offer and acceptance

Consideration

The term "consideration" refers to what each party to a contract does or gives in exchange for what the other party does or gives. In the case of an insurance contract, the consideration made by the prospective policyholder (the applicant) is the submission of the application for insurance and the payment of the premium. The consideration made by the insurer is its promise to pay the benefits described in the policy. For a contract to be valid, consideration must be made by each party to the other.

Meeting of the Minds

The parties to a contract must reach a "meeting of the minds"—that is, both parties must have the same understanding of the agreement and of their respective obligations and rights under the contract.

This concept has a number of implications. "Meeting of the minds" requires that both parties have **good faith**. Good faith on the part of a party means that the party does not have the intention of deceiving or taking unfair advantage of the other party. Without good faith, the parties do not truly have the same understanding of the agreement and so a meeting of the minds has not been reached. Therefore, if it can be shown that either party was not acting in good faith, the contract can be declared invalid and **rescinded** (cancelled).

Sometimes there is no meeting of the minds because important information is missing or incorrect, meaning that through no fault of his own one of the parties does not have an accurate understanding of the terms of the agreement. For example, if the medical history submitted by the policyholder is inaccurate, the insurer will not have a clear understanding of the risk. Or if the explanation of benefits is not clear and accurate, the policyholder will not have a clear understanding of what he may expect in the event of a loss. Although such cases can result from bad faith and the intent to defraud, they may also result from an honest mistake. In either case, a party may seek a modification or a rescission of the contract.

Capacity to Contract

To form a valid contract, both parties must have the ability to understand its terms. Without this capacity there can be no meeting of the minds. Persons are assumed to have this capacity unless they are minors or determined by a court to be mentally incompetent.

Offer and Acceptance

"Offer and acceptance" means simply that one party makes an offer and the other party accepts it. For example, a prospective policyholder may make an offer to buy insurance by submitting an application for a certain policy and paying the premium. The insurer may accept this offer by approving the application, accepting payment, and issuing the requested policy.

Alternatively, the insurer may reject the applicant's offer and end negotiations. Or the insurer may reject the offer by making a counteroffer, so that negotiations continue. For example, the insurer may reject the application by a certain person for a standard policy but propose instead a modified policy (for example, with a higher premium rate or with a special exclusion). The applicant may then accept or reject the counteroffer. Whenever an offer or counteroffer is made, the second component—acceptance by the other party—must occur for the creation of a binding contract.

It may seem odd to think of the applicant as making the offer—after all, don't insurers usually offer their products (insurance policies) to potential customers, who accept or refuse? It is true that the insurer is proposing its product to the customer. But legally, there is a distinction between proposing something and making an offer. A proposal is not technically an offer unless the party making the proposal has taken all necessary actions so that if the other party takes action, that action can constitute acceptance, meaning that the contract is formed. The legal definition of an offer can perhaps best be grasped by keeping in mind that an offer is always potentially the next to last "turn" in the back-and-forth negotiations between parties. Once the offer is made, the other party has the option of taking action that finalizes the contract. If this is not the case, the proposal made is not an offer. Thus when an insurer markets its products, it is not technically making an offer but rather inviting potential policyholders to make an offer by submitting an application.

The Contract, the Policy, and the Application

The words "insurance contract" and "insurance policy" are often used interchangeably in the insurance industry. However, there is a distinction. An insurance contract normally consists of both the policy written by the insurer and the application for insurance submitted by the policyholder.

The policy contains information about the terms of the coverage that the insurer will provide. These terms, expressed in the provisions of the policy, which are also the provisions of the contract, will be discussed in detail in the following chapters.

The application contains information about the prospective policyholder, which she furnishes to the insurer for underwriting purposes. Underwriting is the process whereby an insurer evaluates the circumstances of the applicant, decides whether or not to provide coverage to the applicant, and determines the terms of any coverage that it will provide. (Underwriting is the subject of Chapters 15 and 16.)

In other words, in the application the applicant is making statements that the other party to the contract, the insurer, is basing decisions on. Such statements are known as **representations**. If representations made by the applicant are false, that is, if the information supplied in the application is inaccurate or incomplete, the insurer may rescind the contract. However, if an answer on the application is clearly ambiguous or incomplete, it is the insurer's responsibility to obtain clarification at the time of underwriting and before it issues the policy. If the insurer does not obtain clarification before issuing the contract in such a case, it may not have the right to rescind the policy later, even if it learns that the ambiguous answer contained false information.

Aside from the application, there are other ways in which the contract and the policy are not identical. For example, a contract may exist even if no policy has been issued, if the actions of the parties and the documents involved otherwise satisfy the legal requirements for the existence of a contract. Also, there may be no legally binding contract even if a policy has been issued if either party fails to meet any of the essential elements for the formation of a contract.

Legal Principles of Health Insurance Contracts

Legal Characteristics of Health Insurance Contracts

Health insurance contracts are unilateral, conditional, and aleatory. They are also considered contracts of adhesion.

Unilateral contracts. In a unilateral contract only one of the parties makes a promise. Health insurance contracts are unilateral because only the insurer makes promises. The insurer promises to reimburse the insured for stipulated losses, but the policyholder makes no promise to do or to pay anything. Of course, the policyholder must pay premiums if he wants the policy to continue, but he has not promised to do so. If he stops paying premiums, the policy will lapse, but the insurer cannot sue the policyholder for failure to perform under the contract.

Conditional contracts. Health insurance contracts are conditional because they provide that the insurer will pay the benefits provided by the policy only on the condition that an event insured against occurs. That is, performance under the contract is conditional upon the occurrence of a covered loss.

Aleatory contracts. Health insurance contracts are also aleatory. Under an aleatory contract one of the parties may recover a great deal more in value than she has parted with, depending upon the occurrence of some future contingent event. For example, under a disability income policy the insured could sustain a serious injury after the payment of only one premium and become entitled to total disability benefits and waiver of subsequent premiums for many years.

Contracts of adhesion. Insurance contracts are considered contracts of adhesion—that is, contracts that are offered on a take-it-or-leave-it basis by a party of superior strength and knowledge (the insurer) to a party of limited resources and little expertise (the policyholder).

Court Interpretation of Insurance Policy Language

The courts follow certain principles in interpreting the language of insurance policies. As mentioned above, insurance contracts are considered contracts of adhesion, in which the parties do not have equal bargaining power. Therefore, when there is a dispute between a policyholder and an insurer over the meaning of a contract, the courts generally interpret the contract in a manner that is most favorable to the policyholder.

In addition, certain state courts have developed a theory of contract interpretation called the **doctrine of reasonable expectations**. This doctrine, applied primarily to insurance contracts, holds that, in a dispute over the meaning of a contract, the actual language of the contract may not be the determining factor. If circumstances suggest that the policyholder expected something different from what the written contract states, and if the court considers the policyholder's expectations more reasonable than the conclusion arrived at by strict adherence to the contract language, the court must find in favor of the policyholder.

Legal Requirements for Policy Language

Most states have enacted legislation requiring that some (or all) insurance policies meet certain minimum readability standards. Also, in most states the state insurance department must approve the language used in health insurance policies. The intent of these regulations is to ensure that the language and format of policies are understandable to the average consumer. Regulations vary substantially from state to state.

Definitions in the Insurance Contract

For a meeting of the minds to occur—that is, for both parties to have the same understanding of the agreement they are entering into—the meaning of the language of the contract must be clearly defined. Therefore, contracts include definitions of key words and phrases. Without these definitions, each party might attach its own meanings to terms, and the parties might have very different ideas of such things as what constitutes treatment or who is a dependent.

Different insurers define some of the same terms differently. Other definitions vary little from policy to policy. Common definitions have also changed over time. This change has resulted from legislation, court decisions, and insurance industry efforts to provide more liberal coverage. For example, the definition of a physician originally recognized only those licensed to practice medicine and surgery. Later, laws required insurers to cover services provided by licensed medical practitioners such as psychologists, chiropractors, and advanced practice nurses (on the condition that the services they provided were within the scope of their licenses). The definition of physician in health insurance contracts now reflects this change.

Contract Execution

For an insurance contract to be finalized, several steps must be taken.

First, the applicant signs the application in the presence of a representative of the insurer, usually an insurance agent. (The role of the insurance agent will be discussed in Chapter 11.) The agent witnesses the applicant's signature with his own signature, both to attest that the applicant signed the application in his presence and to fulfill the regulatory requirement of some states that the agent be identified in the application. The applicant then gives the application to the agent.

The agent does not make the decision whether or not to provide insurance. Rather, he passes the application to the insurer. The insurer submits the application to its underwriting process and ensures that all legal requirements are met.

If the outcome of the underwriting process is that the insurer decides to offer a policy to the applicant, an authorized executive officer of the insurer signs the policy. In modern policy issue systems the signature is a facsimile printed on the policy.

Where it is required by law or by the terms of the policy, the next step is the agent's countersignature on the cover of the policy. Even where this signature is not a legal requirement, an insurer may wish to require it to prove the identity of the agent and to make his participation a matter of record (which, it is hoped, will make him exercise care in carrying out his responsibilities). This requirement also helps ensure that insurance sales will be conducted only by agents licensed to do so in the state.

When the policy is signed and countersigned, it is delivered to the applicant. By submitting this signed policy to the applicant, the insurer is making a legally binding offer; if the applicant accepts, a contract will be formed and both parties will be bound by its terms, provided that all contractual requirements are met.

Contract Renewal and Revision

Contract Term and Renewal

An insurance contract is for a stipulated period of time, the term of the policy. Most health insurance policies are renewable—that is, at the end of the original term the policy may be continued. However, certain accident policies and other health insurance coverages designed to cover short-term risk situations are not renewable. They are issued for a single term and must terminate at the end of that term.

Contract Revision

Policyholders often wish to change the type or levels of benefits of a policy and may want changes in other provisions as well. A contract change can be made by means of a **rider**, a document added to a contract to modify or amend the contract. (The terms **"endorsement"** and **"amendment"** mean the same as rider, and the three terms are used interchangeably.) Both parties must agree to the change by signing the rider.

Emerging Trends

The responsibility of insurance company employees and representatives to ensure that their contracts are in compliance with the insurance laws of the states in which they operate has been considerably complicated by the trend toward mergers, acquisitions, joint ventures, and the development of subsidiary companies. Insurer personnel must now develop and file contracts for new corporate entities that may be operating in many different states.

Summary

An insurance contract is a legal agreement between an insurer and a policyholder. The words "policy" and "contract" are often used interchangeably, but they are not exactly the same thing. Health insurance contracts differ greatly, but they all have some things in common. They all must have the four basic elements of a contract (consideration, meeting of the minds, capacity to contract, and offer and acceptance) to be legally binding. Their language and provisions must comply with the regulations of the state where they are issued. They are all considered to be unilateral, conditional, and aleatory contracts and contracts of adhesion. They all have similar procedures for execution, renewal, and revision. Within this common framework, however, a wide variety of contracts are written to meet the diverse needs of consumers.

8 PROVISIONS OF MEDICAL EXPENSE INSURANCE CONTRACTS

- **The Definition of a Dependent**
- **General Provisions**
- **Provisions Related to Premiums**
- **Provisions Related to Benefits and Claims**
- **Provisions Related to the Beginning and End of Coverage**

Introduction

This chapter and the two following chapters will describe the most common and important provisions of the contract for one type of insurance—medical expense insurance. Examining these provisions will give the reader a general understanding of all health insurance contracts, as they contain many of the same provisions. However, it should be kept in mind that contracts for other coverages (such as disability income, accidental death and dismemberment, and long-term care) also contain provisions specific to those coverages.

This chapter will cover provisions common to all medical expense insurance policies, both group and individual. The next chapter will examine provisions specific to group coverage, and the following chapter will examine provisions specific to individual policies.

The Definition of a Dependent

As explained in the previous chapter, to ensure a common understanding on the part of both parties, insurance contracts include definitions of terms. An important definition is that of "dependent," since many policies provide coverage to the dependents of the policyholder (or of the employee in the case of group insurance).

The definition of "dependent" varies little from policy to policy. A **spouse** is typically defined as the person to whom the policyholder or employee is legally married under the laws of the state of residence. However, in some contracts spouse may be defined to include a domestic partner. A spouse is not considered a dependent in cases of legal separation, and a spouse is not covered when he is on active service in any branch of the armed forces or merchant marine of any country.

A **child** must fit one of the following descriptions:

- Under age 19, unmarried, and principally dependent on the policyholder or employee for support.
- Over age 19 but under age 23 (in some cases under 26) and a registered full-time student. Some policies require the child to be legally residing with the policyholder or employee; others require her to be financially dependent.
- Incapable of self-sustaining employment by reason of mental retardation or a physical handicap. In this case the child can be any age, but she must have become incapable prior to attaining the age limit in the contract.

Children may include stepchildren.

General Provisions

Entire Contract Clause

All contracts have an "entire contract clause." This clause states that the present contract, together with any specified attachments, makes up the entire contract and there are no other documents that are part of the contract. In a health insurance contract, the policy and the application of the policyholder (as well as applications of insured persons, if required in the case of group policies) are the entire contract between the policyholder and the insurance company.

Authority to Modify the Contract

Policy provisions may be modified only by agreement between the policyholder and the insurance company. The contract specifically designates those who have the authority to modify it on behalf of each party. Usually, the authorized persons for the insurance company are the officers of the company. Brokers, agents, or other representatives of the insurer do not have the right to make changes in contract provisions.

Consideration Clause

As explained in the previous chapter, all contracts require that the parties exchange a consideration, that is, give up something of value or promise to give up something of value. In the consideration clause, the insurer states that it is issuing the policy (its consideration) in exchange for the application and the payment of the first premium on or before delivery of this policy (the consideration of the policyholder).

Provisions Related to Premiums

Frequency of Premium Payments

A provision of the contract states the frequency of premium payments. Most group policyholders pay premiums monthly, although some plans have annual, semiannual, or quarterly premiums. Individual policies have a variety of payment frequencies, and policyholders can often choose among options.

Premium Rates

Most policies guarantee initial premium rates for 12 months unless the terms of the policy are changed. Occasionally, however, rates are guaranteed for as little as three months or as long as two or three years. After the initial guarantee period, rates may usually be changed only at certain times. Practices vary, but typically rates may be changed on any premium due date (provided the insurer notifies the policyholder at least 31 days before the premium due date) or when the terms of the policy are changed.

Renewal Premium Rates

When a policy is renewed, premium rates sometimes change. Insurers usually do not modify the policy document but rather notify the policyholder of the new rates in a letter or in some other written notice.

The Grace Period for Payment of Premiums

If a policyholder stops paying premiums, the insurer may terminate the contract and stop coverage. However, contracts provide for a grace period. This is a period (commonly 31 days) after the due date of the premium during which the insured's coverage remains in force even if the premium has not been paid. The insurer may not stop coverage during the grace period unless the policyholder has notified the insurer in writing that she is terminating the contract. However, if by the end of the grace period the overdue premium has still not been paid, the contract may be terminated.

If the policyholder pays the overdue premium before the grace period is over, she does not have to pay an interest penalty. On the other hand, for group policies, if the policyholder does not pay the premium by the end of the grace period and the insurer terminates the contract, the policyholder still has the obligation to pay the premium for the grace period, since coverage was in force and the insurer was liable for claims.

Provisions Related to Benefits and Claims

Insuring Clause

The insuring clause expresses in general terms the insurer's promise to pay benefits. It identifies the insurer, states that the insurer agrees to pay the benefits described in the policy to each individual who is insured and who, according to the terms of the policy, is entitled to the benefits, and recites in very general terms the scope and limits of coverage. The clause also specifies that proof of loss must be submitted to the insurer before claim payment will be made.

Benefit Provisions

The benefit provisions section explains in detail each benefit provided by the policy. It states under what conditions the insurer will have the obligation to pay benefits, how the payment will be made, and what the benefits will be. It states any limitations or exclusions. Common benefit provisions for different kinds of coverages are described in the preceding chapters on health insurance coverages.

Claims Payments

The health insurance statutes of some states require that insurers include provisions on claims payment in all health insurance policies. These provisions generally relate to:

- the time limit for submitting a claim to the insurance company (usually 20 days from date of loss);
- the time limit for submitting proofs of loss (usually 90 days from date of loss); and
- the time that the insurance company has to make payment (usually 60 days after proof of loss has been filed).

Coordination of Benefits (COB)

In many families both husband and wife are employed, and each has employer-sponsored group medical insurance that covers dependents. Some people have one or more individual health insurance policies. Consequently, an increasing number of people are insured under more than one health insurance plan, and it can occur that a single medical expense may be covered by more than one policy. This is known as **overinsurance**. If claims are filed with two insurers for the same expense, the insured may receive more in benefits than he actually spent on expenses. This gives the insured an incentive to use more services than he really needs, which increases costs to the insurer, making it necessary for the insurer to raise premiums.

A coordination of benefits (COB) provision addresses this problem. It takes into account the total benefits paid to a person who has overlapping coverage under more than one policy and ensures that the total benefit payments he receives never exceed his total expenses. However, COB provisions in most group policies do not coordinate with individual policies. Coordination of benefits is covered in greater detail in the AHIP book *Health Insurance Nuts and Bolts.*

Assignment of Benefits

Medical expense insurance contracts normally stipulate that the insurer pays benefits directly to the insured. However, most contracts include a provision permitting the insured to assign benefits to the providers of medical care services. This means that, for example, instead of the insurer paying benefits to the insured, who then pays his doctor, the insured can request that the insurer pay the doctor directly. The insurer is not obligated to make the assignment of benefits unless the insured submits a written request to the home office. In practice, however, insurers encourage the assignment of benefits by making it easy to request on claim forms. Insurers often allow and encourage assignment of benefits even if there is no provision in the contract requiring them to do so.

Unassigned Benefits

A provision usually states what occurs if the insured person dies while some benefits remain unpaid. Unassigned benefits usually are paid to the surviving spouse, to any surviving children, or to the executors or administrators of the insured's estate.

Provisions Related to the Beginning and End of Coverage

Effective Date

The effective date of a policy is the date on which the insured begins to be covered by the policy.

The Right to Terminate the Contract

An insurer may terminate a contract on any premium due date only on or after the first policy anniversary. The insurer must give 31 days' advance notice. A group policyholder may terminate its policy on any premium due date, but it also must give 31 days' advance notice. Individuals terminate insurance contracts simply by stopping payment of premiums.

Summary

All medical expense policies, whether they cover a group or an individual, contain certain clauses, definitions, and provisions. These include:

- the entire contract clause, which clearly establishes what documents make up the contract;
- the consideration clause, which states the consideration that each party to the contract is making;
- the insuring clause, which expresses the insurer's promise to pay benefits;
- provisions stating what benefits will be provided and under what conditions they will be provided; and
- provisions stating the amount and frequency of premiums.

Taken together, these articles of the contract clearly establish the rights and obligations of both the insurer and the insured.

9 PROVISIONS OF GROUP MEDICAL EXPENSE INSURANCE CONTRACTS

- *One Policy or Multiple Policies?*
- *The Group Application*
- *Enrollment of Insureds*
- *Beginning of Coverage*

- *Administrative Responsibilities*
- *Experience Refunds*
- *Termination and Continuation of Coverage*

Introduction

In a group insurance policy, the insurer provides coverage to a large group of people. The group can be the members of a union or association, but most often it is the employees of a business. The business (the employer) procures the insurance for the employees and usually pays a portion (or all) of the premiums. Therefore, in group insurance, the contract is usually between the insurer and the employer. The employer is the policyholder, and he acts on behalf of the insureds (the employees).

This chapter describes the provisions particular to group medical expense insurance. In it, the policyholder is usually referred to as the employer and the insureds as the employees. However, the information also generally applies when the policyholder is an association or union and the insureds are members.

One Policy or Multiple Policies?

Employers usually provide their employees with several types of insurance coverage, which together make up the employer's group insurance plan. These types are called **lines of coverage**. There is some variation among insurance companies, but the major lines are usually considered to be the following: life insurance, medical insurance, accidental death and dismemberment insurance, dental insurance, disability income insurance, and long-term care insurance.

An insurer may issue a separate policy to the employer for each major line of coverage included in the plan. Alternatively, the insurer may include all lines of coverage in one policy. This latter approach avoids duplication of policy provisions that are common to all coverages.

Even when multiple policies are issued, some coverages may be combined into one policy. Supplemental major medical insurance is usually written as part of a hospital expense policy (unless they are provided by two different insurers). Dental insurance may also be written as a supplemental benefit under a major medical plan.

The Group Application

For group medical expense insurance, there is a long and a short form of the application for insurance. In the long form the employer provides the information necessary for underwriting, including information on the employees to be covered and the types and amounts of coverage desired. These details are not required in the short form; instead they are provided to the insurer's underwriters on worksheets completed by an agent of the insurer.

Enrollment of Insureds

In group insurance, the policyholder and the insured are not the same. The policyholder is an employer (usually a business), a union, or an association. The insureds are the business's employees or the members of the union or association. So that there is a clear understanding by the insurer and the policyholder of which individuals are covered by the policy, employees or members must be enrolled, that is, they must be officially recorded as being covered.

Sometimes an employer provides some or all coverages to all employees without requiring them to contribute to the cost. In such cases, all employees are automatically enrolled and covered by the policy. However, for record-keeping purposes employees are usually required to fill out **enrollment cards**.

In other plans, employees may choose whether or not to receive coverage and pay a portion of the premium. In this case, the employee requests coverage by completing an enrollment card that includes authorization for payroll deductions, the usual method used by the policyholder to collect employee contributions.

Minimum Enrollment Requirements

When employees have the option of enrolling in a coverage or not, the insurer usually requires, as a condition of beginning and continuing coverage, that a minimum number of employees be enrolled. The requirement may be a percentage of all employees eligible to participate in the plan (such as 75 percent), or a numerical minimum (such as 10 employees), or both. For an association or union, different participation requirements may apply; a minimum requirement of 10 participants is not unusual.

The most common reason for an insurer's termination of a group policy is the failure to meet or maintain minimum enrollment requirements.

Beginning of Coverage

Effective Date

As explained in the previous chapter, the date on which the insureds begin to be covered by a policy is known as the effective date. The effective date of a group contract is established by agreement between the policyholder and the insurer. Usually, this date is shown on the face page of the policy and applies to all of its sections unless there is a special arrangement to have one or more of the coverages become effective at some later date. When an insurer takes over the coverage of a group from another insurer, the effective date of the new contract immediately follows the termination date of the old one so that continuous coverage is provided to the insureds.

Eligibility Date

In some cases, people who join a covered group after the effective date (such as new employees) are not eligible for coverage during a probationary waiting period. This period typically lasts from one to three months, and is designed to eliminate the cost of maintaining records for employees who do not stay with an employer for very long. It must not be so long that it prevents a continuing flow of new entrants into the group.

Employees become eligible for coverage the day after the probationary period ends, their eligibility date. If coverage is automatically extended to all employees, the employee's coverage begins on his eligibility date, although the employee must fill out an enrollment card. If coverage is optional, it can take effect any time on or after the employee's eligibility date, as soon as the employee has filled out an enrollment card and authorized payroll deductions.

If an employee chooses to join a group plan within 31 days of her eligibility date, under most contracts she will be accepted automatically. If she does not join at that time and wants to join later, she is considered a **late entry** (or **late applicant**) and may have to provide **evidence of insurability**. (That is, she may have to provide health and other information proving that she is an acceptable insurance risk.) This is to prevent a person from seeking insurance only after she has contracted an illness. Such a case is another example of adverse selection, explained previously in relation to flexible benefit plans.

Administrative Responsibilities

Some of the work of administering a group health plan is done by employees of the group policyholder. The contract stipulates the responsibilities of the insurer and of the policyholder in this area. Administrative responsibilities of the policyholder's personnel vary, but may include:

- preparing premium statements;
- processing enrollments and terminations;
- issuing certificates of insurance;
- certifying eligibility for coverage when there is a claim; and
- processing claims for medical care benefits in some cases.

Record Keeping

The contract stipulates which party, the insurer or the policyholder, has responsibility for maintaining records on the insured. Information maintained includes names, ages, amounts of insurance, and effective dates of coverage.

Information on Insureds

The policyholder must provide the insurer with certain information on new insureds (such as new employees). The policyholder must also furnish information on changes in classification or status of covered individuals if these changes affect their coverage.

Errors and Benefits

If an error or omission occurs in the record keeping of a group policy, benefits are based on the correct information, not on the error. For example, if a person's age is incorrectly stated in the records, his benefits and premiums will be based on his real age. Moreover, even if a policyholder fails to report to the insurer the termination of an individual's coverage (as when an employee leaves his job), the coverage does in fact terminate.

Experience Refunds

An insurer bases the premium rate it charges a group on its prediction of the cost of providing benefits to that group. Sometimes the actual experience of the group diverges significantly from the insurer's prediction. For example, if claims are much lower than the insurer predicted, the insurer will take in much more in premiums than it pays in claims. An experience refund provision states that if this occurs, the policyholder will be given a refund.

Whether an experience refund must be paid is based on data as of the policy anniversary date, and usually the refund is paid only if the contract is in force and premiums have been paid as of that date. However, policyholders who transfer to another insurer on a date other than the policy anniversary may also be eligible for a refund based on experience up to that time. The experience refund may be in cash, applied to subsequent premiums, or left on deposit with the insurer.

Termination and Continuation of Coverage

Termination of a Group Member's Coverage

In an employer-sponsored group plan, the employee's coverage is normally terminated when:

- the employee ceases to be employed by the policyholder;
- the employee remains employed by the policyholder, but changes jobs so that she is no longer in a class of employees eligible for coverage under the plan;
- the employee (or the policyholder) stops paying premiums;
- the group policy is terminated; or
- the group policy is amended so that the class of employees to which the employee belongs is no longer eligible for coverage.

In a union or association group policy, coverage terminates when membership terminates.

The coverage of an employee's dependent terminates when the employee's insurance terminates, or when the dependent no longer meets the policy's definition of an eligible dependent (such as when a child becomes an adult or when spouses are legally separated).

Coverage Continuation Under COBRA

Under the federal **Consolidated Omnibus Budget Reconciliation Act of 1985 (COBRA),** employers of 20 or more employees are required to include a coverage continuation provision in their group medical benefit plans. This provision must give an employee whose employment is terminated for any reason other than gross misconduct the right to continue coverage for up to 18 months. The continued coverage is paid by the employee. The right of continuation also applies to:

- employees whose employment is not being terminated, but whose hours are being reduced so that they are no longer eligible for coverage;
- spouses and other dependents who lose their eligibility for coverage due to divorce (or legal separation) from the employee, the death of the employee, or the employee becoming eligible for Medicare; and
- dependent children who become ineligible as dependents under the provisions of the plan.

Dependent continued coverage lasts up to 36 months.

Coverage During Family and Medical Leave

The federal **Family and Medical Leave Act of 1993** gives eligible employees the right to take 12 work weeks of unpaid leave during a 12-month period for any of the following reasons:

- the birth of a child or the arrival of an adopted or foster child;
- the care of a child, spouse, or parent who has a serious health condition; or
- a serious health condition of the employee himself that prevents performance of his job.

The act also requires that any employee who is out on family or medical leave must continue to be enrolled in a health insurance plan during that leave.

Conversion Privilege

A conversion privilege gives employees and dependents whose coverage under a group medical expense policy terminates the right to continue coverage on an individual basis. Conversion is permitted under any of the situations cited above under "termination of a group member's coverage." However, the person requesting conversion must also meet both of the following conditions:

- He must have been insured under the group policy for at least three months.
- He must be leaving the group policy and not be eligible for similar coverage under another group plan.

In addition, under some state laws the insured may only take advantage of the conversion privilege after any applicable continuation of coverage has expired.

The person taking advantage of the privilege of conversion is not required to give evidence of insurability. However, he must usually apply in writing and pay the first premium within 31 days of termination of the group coverage.

Summary

Group health insurance policies are purchased by an employer for its employees or by a group for its members. This arrangement entails a number of situations that do not arise in individual insurance, such as the responsibilities of employers in administering the policy, the enrollment of group members in the policy, and the termination of a group member's coverage. The provisions of group policies address these situations and clarify the rights and obligations of insurer, policyholder, and insured.

10 PROVISIONS OF INDIVIDUAL MEDICAL EXPENSE INSURANCE CONTRACTS

- *The Individual Application*
- *Schedule of Benefits*
- *Notice of the Right of Examination*
- *Effective Date*
- *Renewal Provisions*

- *Model Laws*
- *Provisions Required by the Uniform Policy Provisions Law (UPPL)*
- *Optional Provisions of Individual Policies*

Introduction

The parties to an individual insurance contract are, as in a group contract, the insurer and the policyholder. However, in individual insurance the policyholder is not a business, union, or association, but a private individual. This individual is purchasing coverage for herself and in many cases for her dependents.

This chapter will describe those provisions specific to individual medical expense insurance contracts.

The Individual Application

The application for an individual medical expense insurance policy has three sections:

- In Part One, the applicant identifies herself and any other persons proposed for coverage (such as dependents) by name, address, and date of birth.

- In Part Two, the applicant provides information about the coverage she desires, including the type of policy and the nature, amount, and duration of benefits she desires.
- In Part Three, the applicant supplies information needed for underwriting. This information primarily relates to the past medical history of those to be insured. It also covers other risk factors, other insurance coverage that the insured may have, and the insured's occupation and earnings.

The applicant is expected to be able to answer some questions with complete accuracy (for example, when she last consulted a physician or whether she was ever told she had a specific disease). Other questions only require an answer that is accurate to the best of the applicant's knowledge. The application contains a statement that the applicant must sign, attesting that the information provided is true to the best of the applicant's knowledge and belief.

Schedule of Benefits

To make benefit provisions clear and easily understandable to the individual policyholder, a separate schedule of benefits (or policy specifications page) is often used. The schedule of benefits shows the policy number and date of issue, the name of the insured, the initial premium, the various types and amounts of benefits, any maximum benefit periods, any elimination periods, and any other variables.

Notice of the Right of Examination

A notice of the right of examination must appear on the front page of an individual policy. This notice alerts the policyholder to the provision that gives him the right, after he has paid the premium and received the policy, to examine the policy and choose not to buy the coverage. The period during which he may exercise this right is typically 10 days, and the provision is also known as the **10-day-free-look provision**.

Effective Date

Customarily, individual coverage becomes effective after the first premium is paid and the policy is delivered to the applicant. Except in a few states that do not permit it, there may also be a provision stating that coverage will not become effective unless the applicant is in good health at the time of policy delivery.

Renewal Provisions

Most individual medical expense policies are renewable—that is, they can be continued after the initial term. Renewable policies fall into four basic categories, according to the rights of the policyholder to renew:

- noncancellable
- guaranteed renewable
- non-renewable for stated reasons only
- optionally renewable

Noncancellable

Noncancellable is the category that gives the policyholder the most rights. He has the right to continue the same coverage simply by continuing to pay premiums on time. As long as he pays the premiums, the insurer cannot cancel or refuse to renew the policy, make any unilateral changes in any provisions of the policy, or raise the premium rates. However, noncancellable policies often become cancellable when the insured reaches a certain age, usually 50 or older. In the case of a policy issued after age 44, the policy typically is noncancellable for only five years from its date of issue.

Guaranteed Renewable

The policyholder has the same rights under a guaranteed renewable policy as under a noncancellable policy, except that the insurer may make changes in premium rates. However, the insurer may not change the premium rate of a single individual. It can only change the rates of broad categories of people (such as all policyholders of a certain age or occupation).

Nonrenewable for Stated Reasons Only

If a policy is "nonrenewable for stated reasons only," the insurer may refuse to renew, but only under certain circumstances, such as:

- when the policyholder reaches a certain age;
- when the policyholder ceases to be employed; or
- when the insurer nonrenews all policies bearing the same form number as the policyholder's policy.

Optionally Renewable

Under an optionally renewable policy, the *insurer* has the option of renewing the policy, but the policyholder has no right to force the insurer to do so. The insurer has the unilateral right to refuse to renew the policy on any premium due date. Often, instead of flatly refusing to renew, the insurer may set conditions for renewal. Such conditions could include adding policy amendments eliminating coverage for certain types of losses, eliminating coverage for injuries to certain parts of the body, or limiting the extent of coverage for certain occurrences.

Nonrenewal vs. Cancellation

Nonrenewal of a policy is not the same as cancellation of a policy.

- **Nonrenewal** means that on the dates set by the contract for the exercise of the option of renewing the policy, the insurer chooses not to renew. These dates are typically the end of the term of the policy and thereafter any premium due date.
- **Cancellation** means terminating the policy at any time, not necessarily on the renewal dates set by the policy. Some states prohibit cancellation, and in any case cancellation is rare.

Advance notice is required for both cancellation and nonrenewal.

If cancellation does occur, it may not be effective on a premium due date. Therefore, the policyholder may have paid a premium for which he did not receive a full period of coverage. In this case the insurer must make a pro-rated refund.

HIPAA and Renewal

Beginning with policies issued on or after July 1, 1997, the Health Insurance Portability and Accountability Act of 1996 (HIPAA) requires most individual medical expense policies to be guaranteed renewable. Insurers are allowed to nonrenew policies subject to this requirement only in specific circumstances such as when the policyholder does not pay premiums, when the policyholder has engaged in fraud or misrepresentation, or when the insurer decides to stop offering the type of coverage provided by the policy. For policies not subject to HIPAA, the traditional renewal arrangements outlined above are still possible.

Model Laws

In the United States, each state writes its own insurance laws and regulations. However, the **National Association of Insurance Commissioners (NAIC),** made up of state insurance commissioners, has developed model laws that it recommends that states adopt. Many states have enacted these model laws, or adopted them in part or with modifications. This has given the insurance laws of the different states some degree of uniformity. However, policies written by different insurers still differ in matters covered by model laws, as each insurer, even while adhering to a model law, may structure its policies differently and use different wording for similar provisions.

The NAIC has developed four model laws that relate to individual health insurance policies.

- **The Uniform Policy Provisions Law (UPPL)** specifies mandatory and optional provisions for use in all health insurance policies.
- **The Individual Accident and Sickness Insurance Minimum Standards Act** designates several categories for basic forms of coverage with required minimum benefit levels for each.
- **The Official Guide for Filing and Approval of Accident and Health Contracts** sets forth standards for policy language, type size, policy provisions, exclusions, and limitations.
- **The Model Life and Health Insurance Policy Language Simplification Act** establishes standards regarding readability.

Provisions Required By the Uniform Policy Provisions Law (UPPL)

The UPPL requires a number of provisions in individual health insurance policies. These include entire contract provisions, dependent definitions, and grace periods similar to those described in the previous chapter on group insurance contract provisions. Other provisions required by the UPPL include the following:

The Time Limit on Certain Defenses and the Incontestable Clause

The **Time Limit on Certain Defenses Provision** of the UPPL states that three years after an individual health insurance policy goes into effect, the insurer no longer has the right to rescind the policy because of misstatements in the application. Misstatements refer to incorrect information supplied by the policyholder or information that she omitted that was relevant to determining risk. If the misstatements were fraudulent (that is, if the policyholder knowingly made them with the intent to defraud), the time limit does not apply, but fraud can be difficult to prove.

The UPPL's **Incontestable Clause** limits an insurer's right to contest a policy to two years after the effective date and is used in noncancellable or guaranteed renewable policies.

Both the Time Limit On Certain Defenses Provision and the Incontestable Clause also limit to two years an insurer's right to refuse to provide coverage for preexisting conditions except for any that are specifically excluded by name. The obvious advantage of these provisions for insureds is that they offer protection against losing coverage or being deprived of benefits after the contract has been in force for a substantial period of time.

Reinstatement

If the policyholder does not pay an overdue premium before the end of the grace period, coverage ceases. The reinstatement provision sets forth the procedure by which the policyholder can apply for reinstatement of the policy and the insurer can re-evaluate the risk of insuring him. If the policy is reinstated, a 10-day delay provision usually states that illnesses that begin 10 days or less after reinstatement will not be covered.

Claims Provisions

The UPPL has five provisions that deal with the filing of claims:

- The insured must notify the insurer of a loss within 20 days after the loss or as soon as is reasonably possible.
- The insurer must provide claims forms to the insured within 15 days after the insured gives notice of a claim.
- The insured must submit proof of a loss 90 days after the date of the loss, or as soon as is reasonably possible but not later than one year from the end of the 90-day period, except in the absence of legal capacity.
- The insurer must pay claims promptly.
- The insurer must pay the benefits to the insured if living, otherwise to the beneficiary or estate. The insurer may include an optional clause that allows it to pay up to $1,000 to a relative of the insured in the event the insured has died or is incapable of accepting the benefits.

Legal Actions

The insured must wait at least 60 days after submitting proof of loss before starting legal action against the insurer. This provision protects the insurer against lawsuits begun before it has had a reasonable opportunity to investigate a claim. Further, the insured is prohibited from bringing legal action more than three years after the end of the 90-day proof period.

Optional Provisions of Individual Policies

There are several other provisions that state laws generally allow, but do not require, an insurer to include in individual medical expense insurance policies. Some of the most common optional provisions include:

- an adjustment in the amount of the premium if the insured changes to an occupation that is more or less hazardous than the occupation at the time the policy was issued;
- the deduction of an unpaid premium from claim payments; and
- in case of a misstatement of age, the adjustment of the benefit amount to what the premium paid would have purchased if the insured's correct age had been given.

Summary

Individuals who purchase health insurance for themselves and their families do not usually have the ability to knowledgeably review all the language of an insurance policy, as does a large business or group. Individual policies are written so as to address this problem. A schedule of benefits making benefit provisions clear and easily understandable is usually provided. The individual has the right of examination, allowing him to change his mind even after purchasing a policy. In addition, in most states individual policies conform to model laws that have established consistent and fair standards on such matters as payment of claims, renewals of policies, and contesting of contracts.

11 SALES OF GROUP HEALTH INSURANCE PRODUCTS

- *Participants in Group Insurance Sales*
- *Home Office and Field Offices*
- *The Sales Process for Group Health Insurance*
- *Agents and Brokers*
- *The Role of the Group Representative*

Introduction

The preceding chapters explained the insurance contract, the agreement under which an insurer provides coverage and a policyholder pays premiums. For an insurer to do business, it must persuade individuals, employers, or groups to make such an agreement. That is, the insurer must sell its products, which are insurance policies.

This chapter examines the sale of group health insurance products. The following chapter will cover the sale of individual products, which is different in many respects.

Participants in Group Insurance Sales

Agents

Agents are a typical feature of the insurance industry. An insurance agent is someone who acts for an insurer by selling its products and otherwise representing it. Most agents are independent businesspeople who work under a contract with the insurer. In some cases many agents work together in an agency, and the agents may be employees of the agency. In a few cases, agents are employees of the insurer. Agents are licensed by the state.

An agent who is not an employee of an insurer may contract with many different insurers or may have an exclusive contract with one insurer. An agent's contract with an insurer usually authorizes her to sell the insurer's full line of products.

In return for selling policies (and sometimes providing other services), the agent receives compensation, usually in the form of commissions. Agents working for an agency or exclusively for a single insurer usually also receive office space, clerical and backup services, training, and fringe benefits. (Sales compensation is explained in Chapter 13.)

Brokers

Brokers, like most agents, are independent salespersons. The distinction usually made between agents and brokers is that an agent represents the insurer and a broker represents the prospective policyholder. However, in reality the situation is somewhat more complex. Group brokers do advise and assist employers in buying the best coverage at the best price, and in some cases receive fees from employers for their services. However, when a broker sells an insurer's policy to an employer, he is serving as a representative of the insurer and receives a commission from the insurer, just like an agent. Like agents, brokers are licensed by the state.

Employee Benefit Consultants

Employee benefit consultants are individuals or firms that specialize in group benefit plans for employees. Like brokers, consultants advise employers in finding the right group coverage, and they receive a fee from the employer. The difference is that, in general, while a broker assists his client in purchasing a policy, most consultants focus on making recommendations to the client, which the client may then act on. However, the distinction between consultants and brokers is not clear-cut.

Group Representatives

Group representatives are insurance company employees responsible for the selling and servicing of group insurance plans. Group representatives are usually involved in all phases of the sales process and have many functions, which will be explained below. In some companies the sales and service functions are separated; group representatives deal with sales only and **group service representatives** deal with service.

Home Office and Field Offices

The headquarters of an insurance company is known as the home office or head office. Some sales personnel work in the home office, but most are based in field sales offices. Field sales offices are established in other locations so that salespeople can be closer to customers, and each field office usually serves a defined geographic area. In general, the field sales personnel are directly involved in selling, and the home office sales personnel support the field office personnel with product promotion and development, training, administration, and national account services. Group field sales office personnel generally include group representatives (and sometimes group service representatives), support staff, and a manager who supervises the office and reports to a regional vice president or manager. The size and organization of group sales operations vary widely, but the sales and service activities generally are the same.

The Sales Process for Group Health Insurance

Prospecting

The first step of the group insurance sales process is prospecting—identifying potential policyholders (prospects) and making initial contact with them. Prospecting also includes obtaining the information needed for the next step, designing a policy that meets the needs of a certain prospect.

Prospecting is usually done by agents and brokers. Group representatives may sometimes do direct prospecting of large groups, but their primary role at this stage is working with agents and brokers. This involves informing the agents and brokers about the insurer's products, motivating them to sell them, and providing support as needed.

In some cases, a large employer identifies itself as a prospect by issuing a **request for proposals (RFP).** The RFP notifies insurers that the employer is seeking coverage and invites them to propose a plan. The RFP and accompanying documents also outline the needs and requirements of the employer.

Plan Design and Proposal Preparation

Once a prospect has been identified and information obtained, the decision is made whether to proceed to the next step. This step is designing a health insurance plan to meet the prospect's needs and packaging this plan into a proposal to be presented to the prospect. The insurer's home office makes this decision, but the recommendation of the group representative carries a great deal of weight. The representative must feel that the prospect meets the insurer's underwriting standards (that is, the prospect is a good risk) and that there is a reasonably good chance of making the sale.

If the decision is made to proceed, a plan is designed. Both home office personnel and the group representative are typically involved. They must evaluate the prospect's needs, design a plan to meet those needs, underwrite the plan, and calculate the premium rates. For this, more detailed information about the prospect is needed, including an employee census, a description of any present policy, and the claims and premium experience of the present policy. Information on the business of the prospect, any hazards particular to its activities, the prospect's objectives and financial condition, and any collective bargaining agreements affecting the coverage is also useful.

In designing a plan, insurer personnel may also have to meet **plan specifications** set by the prospect. These specifications may be stated in an RFP or by a prospect's broker or consultant. In either case, the purpose of plan specifications is to ensure that when several proposals are submitted by different insurers, they all have certain points in common. This allows the prospect to make direct comparisons and establish, as objectively as possible, which insurer is offering the best coverage at the best price. Plan specifications vary according to the preferences of prospects and brokers.

Once the plan is designed, it must be packaged into an attractive sales proposal. Again, both home office personnel and group representatives are typically involved. A proposal usually includes the following:

- a brief description of each coverage offered in the plan;
- the premium rates for each coverage; and
- information on the insurer—its financial strength and accomplishments and a list of well-known group policyholders.

For large groups, a **cost illustration** of the plan usually covering a three- or five-year period is included in the proposal. A cost illustration shows what portion of the premium paid is used to pay benefits, expenses, etc., and how much, if any, may be returned to the policyholder as an experience refund. Cost illustrations are usually not made for smaller groups as they are not eligible for experience refunds.

Proposal Presentation

The insurer's group representative may have the opportunity to directly participate in presenting the proposal to the prospect, or he may have to submit the proposal to the prospect's broker or consultant, who will analyze proposals submitted by several insurers and make a recommendation to the prospect. Typically, participation by the insurer's group representatives is allowed only by some small broker-age firms.

In evaluating the proposal the prospect considers both the specifics of the plan design (such as benefits, premium rates, and cost illustration) and the insurer's capabilities, experience, and reputation. If there are plan specifications, the degree of compliance with these specifications is considered.

Closing the Sale

The sale is closed when the prospect signs the application and pays the first month's premium.

Employee Enrollment

The next step after closing the sale is usually enrolling the employees in the plan. If participation in the plan is optional, that is, if employees have the choice of contributing to premiums and receiving coverage or not, enrollment must take place to determine whether a sufficient number of employees will participate, according to the requirements of the contract. Even if employees do not have this option, enrollment is necessary for record keeping.

In many cases the insurer is taking over (usually with some changes) an existing plan that was previously provided by another insurer, and employees are already enrolled. However, a new enrollment is sometimes necessary. If a new coverage (such as dental insurance) is being added to the existing plan, employees must be enrolled in the new coverage. If employee contributions to premiums are being increased, re-enrollment is necessary to give employees the option of participating under the new terms or not, and to determine if a sufficient number of employees will participate. Finally, even when there are no changes in coverage or employee contributions and so re-enrolling employees is not strictly necessary, the insurer may want to do it to help increase employee awareness of the plan and to introduce itself as the new insurer.

Whatever the case, the new plan (or new coverage, or changes in the existing plan) is presented to the employees. The insurer usually prepares an announcement letter or explanatory booklet. The employer's personnel distribute the information and arrange for employee presentation meetings. If enrollment is to take place, employer personnel distribute enrollment cards and follow up to obtain the signed cards. The active support of the employer's personnel is essential to getting back signed employee enrollment cards.

Execution of the Contract and Installation

When the enrollment process has been completed, the insurer's group representative sends the policyholder's signed application, the employee enrollment cards, and the first month's premium to the insurance company's home office or group field office for final acceptance. The home office issues the master policy and sends it along with individual certificates and administrative material to the group representative. The group representative, usually accompanied by the agent or broker, delivers the material to the policyholder and thoroughly reviews all aspects of the plan's administration, including premium billing and accounting, claim procedures, and benefits. Administrative procedures are established and installation occurs (that is, the plan goes into effect). For small and medium-size groups, it is often the agent alone who works with the policyholder in effecting the installation.

Servicing the Policyholder

The group representative or group service representative makes periodic service calls on the policyholder to assist in the proper administration of the plan. The representative customarily uses a check-off type form to make a thorough review of administrative practices and to track the status of various aspects of the plan. He also generally uses this form as a service report to the home office. As with installation, the agent is often given responsibility for providing administrative assistance and continuing service to small and medium-size groups.

The retention of business is an important purpose of providing good service. Regular and efficient service increases the satisfaction of policyholders and makes them more likely to renew a policy. Poorly serviced plans are prime targets for sales efforts by other insurance companies and brokers. In addition, the group representative or agent must maintain close relationships and good communication with policyholders. This allows the representative or agent to address difficulties, such as service problems or a necessary rate increase, that otherwise might cause the policyholder to let a policy lapse or transfer it to another insurer. And as an added benefit, a group representative or agent who maintains good service relationships will increase his opportunities to sell expanded or additional group coverages to his policyholders.

Agents and Brokers

Other Roles of Agents and Brokers

The typical involvement of agents and brokers in different steps of the sales process has been described. However, some variations should be noted.

- Although most insurers both employ group representatives and work through agents, brokers, and consultants, some insurers are too small to employ group representatives. These insurers usually delegate all sales and service responsibilities to contracted agents and brokers.
- Other insurers, known as **direct writers**, do not use agents or brokers at all and only approach prospective policyholders through their salaried employees (group representatives).
- A group broker may act as a **third-party administrator (TPA).** A third-party administrator is a firm that is neither the insurer or policyholder of a group insurance plan that takes responsibility for the administration of that plan. This arrangement is most common in self-insured plans.
- As mentioned, insurers often contract agents to provide service for small and medium-size groups.

Market Share of Agents and Brokers

Most sales of health insurance for small and medium-size groups are made by agents. Large group sales are made primarily by brokers. In this large group market, individual brokers and small general brokerage firms account for a significant portion of sales, but brokers specializing in group health insurance and very large general brokerage firms with specialized group health insurance departments control the largest percentage of the business in terms of premiums paid. The large general firms have the advantage of already serving as advisors to the top management of large companies on other insurance lines (property, casualty, and fire), which gives them contacts in these companies and knowledge of the companies' operations and needs.

The Attraction of Group Sales for Agents

Many agents are attracted to selling group health insurance not only because of the compensation offered by the insurer, but for other reasons as well, including:

- While selling group health insurance, an agent makes contact with prospects for other business insurance or individual insurance.
- If an agent is already selling to business clients, adding group health insurance enables him to offer a complete range of products and service to this market.
- Selling group insurance gives agents the opportunity to sell during the normal nine-to-five workday. (Agents selling individual insurance must sell when individuals are at home.)

The Role of the Group Representative

As we have seen, the group representative is usually involved in every step of the sales process. It will be useful to summarize her role.

The sales responsibilities of the group representative include:

- identifying and contacting prospects and obtaining information about them (usually done through agents and brokers, but large employers may sometimes be contacted directly);
- submitting information about prospects to the home office and making recommendations on proposals;
- preparing proposals and presenting them to prospects (includes working with any brokers and consultants representing the prospect);
- assisting in the closing of sales; and
- keeping the home office informed of competitive developments in the field.

Service responsibilities may be handled by the group representative or in some companies by a group service representative. They include:

- assisting in the enrollment of employees;
- installing the plan and setting up administrative procedures;
- making regular service calls to assist the employer in the administration of the policy and in insurance plan modernization; and
- retaining present policyholders by providing good service and maintaining good communication.

The Group Representative's Relationship with Agents

One of the group representative's most important responsibilities is working with agents and brokers to get them to bring business to the insurer. In the case of full-time agents of the insurer, this means providing them with information, training them, and motivating them to prospect. This involves distributing written information, conducting training sessions, and organizing periodic meetings. The group representative also must establish a close working relationship with each agent, as this is the most effective way to educate and motivate her.

Group representatives also work to develop relationships with independent agents and with brokers so that they will serve as sources of business. As with the insurer's agents, the group representative works to inform, train, and motivate independent agents and brokers and to establish close relationships with them. In dealing with large, specialized brokerage firms and employee benefit consultants, the group representative focuses on demonstrating his own abilities to the broker and convincing him of the superior products and capabilities of his company.

Summary

Agents, brokers, consultants, and insurer employees are all involved in the sales of group health insurance policies. Selling these policies involves the following steps:

- identifying prospects and making initial contact with them;
- designing a health insurance plan to meet the prospect's needs and packaging this plan into a proposal;
- presenting the proposal;
- closing the sale;
- enrolling the group members in the plan;
- executing the contract and installing the plan; and
- providing continuing service to the policyholder and the insureds.

All participants must work together to ensure both that the sale is made and that the policyholder continues the policy.

12 SALES OF INDIVIDUAL HEALTH INSURANCE PRODUCTS

- *Agents and Brokers*
- *Sales Offices and Agencies*
- *The Sales Process for Individual Health Insurance*
- *Direct Sales of Individual Health Insurance*

Introduction

The selling of individual health insurance products, like group product sales, is done largely by agents and brokers. However, while group agents and brokers are able to sell coverage for large numbers of people by working with employers, agents and brokers selling individual products must deal one-on-one with many private individuals who are buying a policy only for themselves or their families. Consequently, the sales process for individual products is in many ways different from the group sales process. This chapter will examine individual sales, highlighting these differences.

Agents and Brokers

Agents

Agents sell individual health insurance products directly to consumers on a person-to-person basis. In the sales process, an agent is the contracted representative of the insurer. As such, he performs other functions for the insurer:

- **Field underwriting.** Agents do initial risk selection—that is, they make preliminary rough judgments about whether and on what terms the insurer would want to insure an individual.

- **Policyholder service.** Agents provide service to existing policyholders, including answering questions and assisting in policy changes.
- **Public relations.** Agents are responsible for projecting the proper image of the insurer to the consumer.

Brokers

Brokers also sell individual health insurance products to the public. Individual brokers, like group brokers, assist the prospective policyholder in finding a policy and insurer that offer the proper coverage at the best price. However, also like a group broker, when an individual broker sells a policy, she is serving as a representative of the insurer and is paid a commission by the insurer. Many brokers sell a full line of property and casualty coverages as well as life and health insurance.

Although most health insurers accept business from individual brokers, some do not. These insurers maintain that since brokers often sell many types of coverage, they do not have the expertise in health insurance they need to provide both knowledgeable service to the consumer and field underwriting assistance to the insurer. However, in recent years many large property and casualty brokerage firms have established separate departments staffed by brokers specializing in life and health insurance. These brokers are just as sophisticated in health insurance and field underwriting as full-time, company-trained health insurance agents.

Sales Offices and Agencies

Agents selling individual health insurance may be connected with an insurer's branch office, a general agency, or a personal producing general agent's office.

The Insurer's Branch Office

An insurer's branch office is a field sales office. It is under the exclusive control of the insurer and is run by a **branch sales manager** who is the insurer's employee. The branch sales manager generally exercises control over several branches and reports to a regional or divisional manager. His responsibilities include the following:

- working with agents to develop and maintain a certain quantity and quality of sales; (This involves disseminating information from the insurer to the agents as well as motivating and supporting agents. Agents may be either employees of the insurer or independent contractors.)
- recruiting and training new agents;
- handling policyholders' service problems;

- supervising office employees; and
- managing the expenses of the office.

The General Agency

A general agent is an independent businessperson who operates her own sales office (a general agency) under contract to an insurer. The agent provides her own office facilities and clerical and supervisory personnel, and recruits, trains, and supervises her own agents. However, the insurer may pay a development expense allowance to a contracted general agent to help pay the agency's overhead expenses. The amount of this payment is usually based on how much business is sold by the general agency and how long it stays in force. The insurer may also share some of the expenses of training and financing new agents.

Personal Producing General Agents (PPGAs)

Personal producing general agents also work as independent businesspersons under contract to an insurer. PPGAs are usually people who, having been successful agents for a number of years, seek contractual relationships that give them, in return for this ability to produce business, greater commission compensation than they received as agents. Most PPGAs have the authority to hire or appoint their own agents and work with brokers. In general, personal producing general agents absorb all their own expenses, including office facilities, clerical staff, and any other overhead expenses, although they usually receive fringe benefits such as group life and health coverages and retirement benefits under the insurer's benefit plans.

The Sales Process for Individual Health Insurance

Prospecting

As with group insurance, prospecting means identifying and contacting prospects and obtaining information about them. A prospect is a potential policyholder, which means he must be more than just a name on a list—he must have a current need for health insurance and the ability to pay for it, and must be able to meet the insurer's underwriting requirements. Nevertheless, agents must usually start with lists of names and from those lists develop a file of true prospects. Names include an agent's friends, relatives, and acquaintances, and the agent's or insurer's present policyholders, who can be sold additional coverages. Names also come from referrals from all of these people and from anyone else who can influence other persons favorably toward the purchase of insurance from a particular agent. Other sources include telephone directories, city and county records, mortgage lists, graduation lists, announcements of marriages and births, and community activity lists. Specialized lists from listing companies that compile and sell them also can be useful.

In addition, some agents specialize in selling to specific professional or ethnic groups. These agents use trade shows, newsletters, and the sponsorship of events targeted to these groups to identify and contact prospects.

Finally, insurance companies use mass marketing methods to identify individual prospects (as described in Chapter 14). These prospects are usually referred to an agent.

The Approach

When an agent has identified a prospect, she contacts the prospect to try to arrange a sales interview. This first contact and attempt to set up an interview is known as the approach. Some of the more common methods are:

- **The cold call.** The agent makes an unannounced visit to the prospect.
- **The telephone call.** The agent telephones the prospect and attempts to create interest in setting up a sales interview.
- **The pre-approach letter.** The agent sends a letter to the prospect to attempt to create interest in an interview. The agent will usually follow up with a visit or telephone call to arrange the interview.
- **The referral.** A mutual friend or associate of the agent and prospect makes an appointment for the agent. Alternatively, a pre-approach letter is sent with a list of people (usually clients) who recommend the agent and are known to the prospect.

Referrals are very important to an agent's business. Especially important are clients who have contact with many persons who respect their opinions. These persons are referred to as **centers of influence**, and may include attorneys, bankers, accountants, or realtors.

The Interview

If the approach is successful, the agent obtains an interview with the prospect. In the interview, the agent tries to learn about the prospect's needs so that she can recommend an appropriate policy. The agent wants to know the answers to two questions:

- What health insurance does the prospect already have?
- Are there any gaps in that health insurance that need to be filled to ensure adequate protection?

The answers to these questions will place the prospect's needs into one of three categories:

- **Primary permanent.** The prospect does not already have an individual health insurance policy, is not covered by an employer's group plan or a government program, and does not expect to be covered in the near future. He needs a primary health insurance policy on a permanent basis. **Primary** means that this will be the prospect's main health insurance coverage, not a supplement to another policy.
- **Primary interim.** The prospect expects to be covered by an employer's group plan soon, usually within one to six months. He needs a primary policy but on a temporary basis. Typically, he is someone who is between jobs, newly employed and so ineligible for group coverage during an initial probationary period, or new to the job market (just out of high school or college or recently discharged from military service).
- **Supplemental.** The prospect is covered by a primary health insurance plan but needs supplemental coverage to cover deficiencies in this plan.

Choosing a Coverage

For each prospect the agent chooses the coverage that meets his needs. For a primary permanent prospect, this will most likely be major medical expense coverage, disability income coverage at a level of protection adequate for the prospect's living expenses, and perhaps long-term care coverage. For a primary interim prospect the agent chooses the same sort of plan, but on a temporary basis. For a supplemental prospect, the agent selects a supplemental policy that fills the gaps in the prospect's current coverage.

Presenting the Recommended Coverage

When the agent has chosen a coverage to recommend, she makes a presentation to the prospect. For this agents generally use promotional material prepared by the insurer. Materials may include brochures, pamphlets, and visual aides for oral presentations. The agent uses the prepared materials to clarify the benefits and limitations of the coverage and then explains how it meets the prospect's individual needs. In this way, the agent provides the prospect with the information he needs to make a decision.

Closing the Sale

The agent closes the sale by obtaining from the prospect a signed application and a prepayment of the first premium, although the latter is not always required.

Servicing the Policyholder

After the insurer accepts the application and issues the policy, the agent often personally delivers the policy to the new policyholder. In any case, the agent meets with the new policyholder, reviews the benefits the policy provides, explains the procedure for submitting a claim, and gives the policyholder a claim form.

The agent should provide efficient and timely service throughout the lifetime of the contract. As with group insurance, a good service relationship makes retention more likely. It also can lead to the policyholder giving the agent referrals of new prospects and the agent selling additional coverage to the policyholder as his needs change.

Direct Sales of Individual Health Insurance

In a few cases insurers sell coverage directly to consumers, without working through agents or brokers. The product sold is usually a supplemental coverage, and the most common example is the sale of travel accident policies, which was described in Chapter Four. In addition, some of the mass marketing methods for individual insurance described in Chapter 14 can result in direct insurer-to-prospect sales, although more often an agent is involved.

Summary

Individual health insurance policies are sold by agents and brokers working in a variety of arrangements. Individual sales involve dealing with large numbers of prospects on a one-to-one basis. Consequently, the individual sales process differs somewhat from the group sales process. The steps of the individual sales process are:

- prospecting (identifying prospects and obtaining information about them);
- making the approach (the first contact during which the agent attempts to set up an interview);
- conducting the interview (during which the agent tries to learn about the prospect's needs);
- choosing a coverage to meet the needs of the prospect;
- presenting the recommended coverage to the prospect;

- closing the sale; and
- providing service to the policyholder.

These activities are all carried out by the agent or broker, with the support of the insurer.

13 SALES COMPENSATION

- *Commissions*
- *Override Commissions*
- *Vesting*
- *Other Compensation for Agents*
- *Broker Fees*
- *Bonuses for Insurer Employees*

Introduction

The preceding chapters described how insurance agents and brokers sell insurers' policies for them, and how agents sometimes also provide services to policyholders on behalf of an insurer. For this, insurers of course compensate agents and brokers, usually by paying them commissions for each sale they make. This chapter will explain in detail the payment of commissions. It will also describe other forms of payment to agents and brokers, as well as the compensation of other sales personnel.

Commissions

The commission is the principal means by which insurers compensate agents and brokers. For the sake of brevity, in the following discussion only agents will be mentioned, but commissions paid to brokers are similar.

A sales commission is a payment made to a salesperson for the sale of a product. In insurance, the commission that an agent receives for the sale of a policy is normally a percentage of the premiums the policyholder pays on that policy. In individual sales, the commission percentage is usually the same regardless of the amount of premiums that the policyholder pays. For example, if an insurer's commission percentage for a certain type of policy is 10 percent, the agent will receive 10 percent whether the policyholder is paying $500 or $1,000 annually. In group sales on the other hand, the commission percentage usually varies accord-

Table 13.1

High-Low and Level Commission Schedule

	High-low scale percentage commission		Level scale percentage commission
Annual premium	1st year	2nd through 10th year	All 10 years
First $1,000	20.0%	5.0%	6.5 %
Next 4,000	20.0	3.0	4.7
Next 5,000	15.0	1.5	2.85
Next 10,000	12.5	1.5	2.6
Next 10,000	10.0	1.5	2.35
Next 20,000	5.0	1.5	1.85
Next 200,000	2.5	1.0	1.15
Next 250,000	1.0	.5	.55

ing to the amount of premiums paid. The percentages for different premium amounts are set forth in a **commission schedule.** (See Table 13.1.)

An agent's commission is a percentage not only of premiums paid during the initial term of the policy, but also of premiums paid in the following years if the contract is renewed. Therefore, an agent derives income not only from her recent sales, but also from renewals of sales she made in previous years.

Two types of commission schedules are in general use: the **high-low commission schedule** and the **level commission schedule**, also known as the high-low and the level scales. The high-low commission schedule pays the agent a higher percentage of premiums during the first year a policy is in force and lower commissions in renewal years. The level commission schedule pays the same percentage every year.

In the long term, an agent does not generally earn more with one type of schedule than with the other. The difference is in distribution over time—more in the first year and less later (for high-low schedules) or the same every year (for level schedules).

Some insurers allow agents to choose the type of schedule, but others do not. Insurers often prefer a level commission schedule because they generally have high expenses during the first year of a contract and a high-low commission schedule adds to these first-year expenses. Also, because a level schedule gives agents greater compensation for renewals, it encourages them to try to retain policyholders by providing good service. High-low schedules, on the other hand, actually give agents an incentive to replace policies and so earn a first-year commission. Furthermore, some insurers and the regulators in some states require a level schedule for group policies in some circumstances, such as the following:

● A group coverage is being transferred from one insurer to another. (This is far more common today than groups being insured for the first time.)

- A group policy is being reinstated.
- The group policyholder is not contributing to premiums (the insureds are paying all of the amount of the premiums).
- A group policy is judged by the insurer to have a high chance of lapse.
- An employer's group policy is negotiated with unions.

In general, the level commission schedule is becoming the more common schedule.

Most insurers pay higher commission percentages for disability income insurance than for medical expense insurance. This reflects the fact that an insurer makes less on medical expense insurance—the ratio of the insurer's claims and administrative expenses to premiums received is higher than for disability income coverages, and medical expense policies have poorer **persistency.** (Persistency is the likelihood that the policyholder will renew the policy year after year.) The higher percentage commissions paid for disability income insurance also reflect the fact that agents spend more time selling these policies. (Persuading consumers of the need for income protection and arriving at the proper amount of coverage can be time-consuming.)

There are other variations in the payments of commissions. Some insurers give the agent an advance by paying the commissions for all of the first-year premiums in one sum as soon after the sale as possible, instead of waiting until the premiums are actually paid. Some insurers pay a slightly higher scale for groups of fewer than 25 employees, since for small groups the agent often does more of the work of selling, installing, and servicing. And some insurers pay a persistency fee if a policy remains in force beyond the tenth policy year.

New agents have not had the time to develop a base of prospects, and they are not receiving renewal commissions from sales made in previous years. Consequently, their income may be low in the first few years. To assist new agents, many insurers pay them advances on future commissions. The maximum amounts and schedules of such advances differ from one insurer to another and are usually only provided to agents selling exclusively for the insurer. Other means of assisting new agents are discussed below.

In summary, an agent's commission on a policy is a percentage of the premiums paid on that policy. This percentage may depend in part on:

- the type of policy sold (disability income vs. medical expense); and
- the length of time the policy has been in force (if a high-low schedule and/or persistency payments apply).

For group insurance, the commission percentage may also depend on:

- the size of the group (if higher percentages for smaller groups are paid); and
- the amount of the premiums.

Table 13.2

Override Commission Schedule

| Annual premium | High-low scale percentage commission | | Level scale percentage commission |
	1st year	2nd through 10th year	All 10 years
First $1,000	4.0%	1.0 %	1.3 %
Next 4,000	4.0	.6	.94
Next 5,000	3.0	.3	.57
Next 10,000	2.5	.3	.52
Next 10,000	2.0	.3	.47
Next 20,000	1.0	.3	.37
Next 200,000	.3	.13	.15
Next 250,000	.2	.10	.55

Override Commissions

In addition to the commission paid to the agent making the sale, an insurer may pay a commission to a general agent or agency manager. This is known as an override commission. It compensates this person for the assistance he provides to the selling agent, assistance that the insurer would otherwise have to provide. Like the selling agent's commission, the override commission can be based on a high-low or a level schedule. (See Table 13.2.)

Vesting

As explained above, an agent normally continues to receive as commissions a percentage of the premiums on a policy she has sold as long as the policyholder continues to pay the premiums, both during the initial term of the policy and during any renewals. What happens when an agent sells a policy for an insurer and then the agent's contract or employment with the insurer terminates? Will the agent continue to receive commissions from the insurer? If the agent's contract gives her vesting rights, the answer is yes. Vesting is the right of an agent to receive commissions payable from an insurance sale even after termination of her contract with the insurer.

Vesting differs among insurers. With some companies, the agent has the right to only a portion of the commissions. Some companies give unconditional vesting rights, while others grant vesting only under certain conditions. These conditions usually relate to how long the agent has been with the insurer, the amount of the agent's sales, and the reason for the agent's termination (such as whether the termination was voluntary or involuntary, or if it was due to death or disability). Commissions may be vested after the agent's death, in which case they are payable to the agent's estate or to a person the agent has designated. The trend in group insurance is away from vesting.

Other Compensation for Agents

Although commissions make up the bulk of an agent's income, other compensation is sometimes provided. (For the sake of brevity only insurers are referred to here, but in some cases this compensation may be provided by agencies.)

Training Allowances for New Agents

As mentioned above, some insurers grant new agents advances on future commissions in their first years when their commissions are low. Other insurers pay a training allowance (a salary) to new agents. The agent is usually required to produce a certain amount of premiums or commissions to justify the allowance. The arrangement may last for a few months or a few years.

Fringe Benefits

An insurer may provide fringe benefits to agents. Generally the agents must be working full-time for the insurer, and most insurers also require that an agent habitually produce a certain amount of business to be eligible. Benefits typically include a group health and life insurance plan, a retirement plan (with contributions made by both the insurer and the agent), and the insurer's Social Security program. The employer pays half the Social Security tax and withholds the other half from the agent's commissions.

Incentives

An insurer may offer extra incentives (in addition to commissions) for high sales. Sales campaigns can be organized to give specified monetary awards for increased levels of production. Agents who meet or exceed pre-set standards of performance may be given the opportunity to go to sales conventions. Such rewards provide not only financial compensation but also the recognition of excellence, and this can help motivate agents to perform at maximum levels.

Broker Fees

Most brokers, like agents, derive their income principally from sales commissions paid by insurers. However, some brokers of group coverage receive a fee from the employers they assist. This fee is not usually based on premiums, but is more likely to be a flat monthly or annual amount or a per-employee-per-month charge. Fees are most common with brokers representing large clients or acting as third-party administrators.

Bonuses for Insurer Employees

Group representatives are employees of the insurer and are paid a salary. They also sometimes receive incentive bonuses for exceeding goals or quotas. The amount is usually a percentage of premiums, either first-year premiums only or both first-year and renewal premiums. The importance of bonuses varies from insurer to insurer, and the amount ranges from 10 to 50 percent of a group representative's salary. Sometimes the total bonus amount cannot be greater than the amount of salary. In cases where total compensation determines the amounts of company fringe benefits due to a group representative, the amounts of bonuses may be included in the calculation.

In the individual sales field, branch sales managers are compensated in much the same way as group representatives are in the group field. They are insurer employees and are paid a salary, but they usually receive additional compensation based on the quantity and quality of sales, the retention of business, and/or the amount of premium that policyholders continue to pay year after year.

Summary

Agents and brokers are compensated for selling insurers' products and providing service to policyholders primarily by means of commissions. They may also receive other compensation, such as training allowances, fringe benefits, and incentive payments. Brokers may also receive fees from the policyholders they assist. Insurer employees are paid salaries, but bonuses may be an important component of their compensation package.

14 MARKETING OF HEALTH INSURANCE PRODUCTS

- *Markets for Group Health Insurance Products*
- *Markets for Individual Health Insurance Products*
- *Mass Marketing of Individual Insurance*
- *Product Research and Development*
- *Trends in the Marketing of Health Insurance Product*

Introduction

What is marketing? In the past, the term "marketing" was nearly synonymous with selling and referred only to salespeople's activities. Specifically, marketing was the salesperson's sales plans and the methods he used to persuade the consumer to buy a product. However, in recent years the concept of marketing has been expanded. It now refers to a wide range of functions, which are performed not just by salespersons but by people from many different departments of a company. These functions generally fall into one of four broad areas:

- identifying a market;
- evaluating the needs of that market;
- developing products to meet those needs; and
- promoting and distributing those products.

In the health insurance industry, a product is a coverage—a policy with a certain combination of benefits, premiums, and other features. So in a health insurance company, the marketing functions are:

- identifying markets for the types of coverage that the company sells;
- researching the precise needs of people who might want to buy that coverage;
- developing insurance policies that meet those needs; and
- promoting and selling those policies.

There is a still broader definition of marketing. Businesspeople now realize that every activity they engage in, by affecting product and service quality, ultimately helps determine whether consumers buy their products. Therefore, in a sense all corporate functions are directly or indirectly related to marketing. In the case of an insurance company, this means that functions such as actuarial science, customer service, and claims service affect product sales or the retention of a policyholder in some way. For example:

- **Actuaries** (insurance mathematicians) analyze numerical data to calculate premium rates, dividends, and reserves and to prepare statistical studies and reports. They must use their abilities to make rates for new and existing products as competitive as possible while maintaining profitability.
- **Customer service personnel** can help retain the business of policyholders who are considering renewal by suggesting premium-reducing options such as an increase in deductibles or a switch to a managed care arrangement.
- **Claims departments** can also increase retention by rewarding policyholders for finding billing errors or reporting suspected fraudulent activities.

In this chapter, we will examine three major topics in the area of health insurance marketing: identification of markets, direct marketing of individual products, and development of new products.

Markets for Group Health Insurance Products

The potential customers for group health insurance products make up a large and diverse market. Insurers divide this market into smaller markets (or market segments) based on the type of policyholder and the size of the insured group.

Types of Group Policyholders

Single employers. A single employer is an employer that is a single legal entity that purchases group coverage for its employees. This entity may be a sole proprietor, a partnership, or (most commonly) a corporation. A single employer may be a collection of legal entities only if these entities are insured through a common owner, as in the case of subsidiary companies all owned by the same corporation. Single employers make up by far the largest share of the group health insurance market, accounting for about 90 percent of all group policies in force.

Multiple-employer trusts (METs). An insurer, agent, broker, consultant, or insurance administrator may arrange for several employers, usually in the same or related industries, to come together and form a trust to purchase health insurance for their employees. The policyholder in this case is the trust. This arrangement creates a large group of insureds, which can make it possible for the insurer to provide coverage at a lower cost and otherwise gives the group of small companies many of the same advantages as a company with a large number of employees.

Trade associations. Employers that are members of a trade association may provide insurance for their employees through the association. The association is the policyholder. This type of arrangement accounts for less than one percent of all group contracts in force.

Professional associations and other individual associations. Individuals in various professions—law, medicine, engineering, and education, for example—sometimes provide group coverage for themselves and in some cases their employees through a policy issued to their professional association or to a trust formed to administer the insurance. Other, nonprofessional associations of individuals may make the same arrangement. Normally in such cases the premium is paid wholly by the individual. Professional and other associations compose a small part of all group contracts in force.

Labor unions. Some national, regional, or local labor unions purchase group policies to provide health insurance coverage for their members. In such cases, the union may use funds from member dues to pay the premiums, or members may pay all or a portion of premiums, as in an employer-sponsored plan. Only a small and declining number of group policies are held by unions. Generally, unions prefer that employers provide group health insurance and try to achieve this through collective bargaining.

Negotiated union-management trusteeships (Taft-Hartley groups). In some cases, one or more unions negotiate group health insurance coverage for their members with one or more employers. The resulting insurance policy is held neither by the employers nor the unions, but rather by a trusteeship established under the authority of the **Labor Management Relations Act of 1947 (the Taft-Hartley Act).** Because this is a federal law, such trusteeships only apply to union members engaged in activities that affect interstate or foreign commerce. Taft-Hartley groups account for about 2 percent of all group insurance contracts in force.

Creditor groups. A lending institution, such as a bank or finance company, may buy a policy to insure itself against nonpayment by persons owing it money due to the death or disability of those persons. (Because it is in a sense disability income insurance, this is considered a form of health insurance.)

Group Size

Insurers also categorize markets for group health insurance products by the size of the insured group. This is expressed in terms of number of **insured lives** (number of people insured).

Small groups (fewer than 100 lives). Small groups account for about 80 percent of all group health insurance policies in force. Purchasers in this category are concerned primarily with cost, simplified administration, and getting the same kinds and quality of benefits that are available to larger groups. Agents make most of the sales to small groups.

Medium-size groups (100 to 500 lives). This category accounts for about 10 percent of all group contracts in force. Purchasers are primarily interested in cost, flexibility of plan design, and quality of service. Compared to small groups, greater flexibility in benefit design and administration can be offered. Agents, brokers, and consultants all actively sell to this market.

Large groups (500 or more lives). This category also accounts for about 10 percent of all group contracts in force. However, due to the large size of the groups, it accounts for over half of the total premium dollars paid. Policies marketed to large groups are often tailored to the specifications of the buyer, and administrative procedures may be modified to suit policyholder needs. Insurers usually sell these contracts through brokers or employee benefit consultants or sometimes directly.

Markets for Individual Health Insurance Products

Insurers sell individual health insurance policies to three consumer groups. These correspond to the three categories of prospect need discussed in the section on the individual sales process in Chapter 12. The three groups are:

- People who depend solely or largely on an individual policy for health insurance protection (need category: primary permanent).
- People who need temporary coverage (need category: primary interim).
- People covered by a primary health insurance plan but needing supplemental coverage to meet deficiencies in their primary plan (need category: supplemental).

Mass Marketing of Individual Insurance

Insurers selling individual health insurance policies normally work with agents and brokers who personally contact consumers one by one. But some insurers also use mass marketing to approach a large number of prospects cheaply and quickly. Mass marketing techniques include direct mail, advertising, third-party sponsorship, franchise plans, and the Internet. If a prospect responds to mass marketing, an insurer employee may contact her and make the sale by mail or by telephone, or the insurer may arrange for an agent to visit the prospect.

Direct Mail

Direct mail marketing involves targeting prospects and sending them information by mail. The mailing usually includes a proposal describing the coverage the insurer is offering and a short-form application (with a minimal number of health and occupation questions) that interested prospects can fill out and mail back to the insurer.

Advertising

Insurers use newspaper and magazine advertisements to approach prospects for policies with limited, easy-to-understand benefits (mainly hospital indemnity or limited medical expense coverage). These advertisements often contain a short-form application. Radio and television advertising can also be used for these policies. In this case viewers and listeners are given a toll-free telephone number to call for additional information or to apply for the coverage.

Third-Party Sponsorship

The third party in this context is a non-insurance business that provides an insurer with access to its customers. It may be a bank, a savings and loan association, or a corporation that uses credit cards or some other regular billing system. Typically, the insurer sends advertisements with the third party's billing or correspondence, or places advertisements in the third party's place of business. If a customer of the third party buys a policy, the third party usually bills the customer for insurance premiums. Otherwise, the insurer handles all transactions related to the policy.

Franchise Plans

Franchise plans (sometimes called **worksite marketing**) are a way of selling individual insurance policies to members of a group (usually an employee group but sometimes an association). It must be emphasized that this is not an example of group insurance, but rather an approach to selling individual insurance. The policyholder is the individual, not an employer or association. While the insurer sells to members of a group, the insurer underwrites each member of the group separately. That is, the insurer decides on a case-by-case basis whether and on what basis to provide insurance to any member of the group who may apply for it. A standard policy may be proposed for the group, but the insurer can decide to modify that policy for some members.

On the other hand, franchise plans do offer individuals some of the advantages of group insurance:

- When an individual policy is obtained through franchise plans, there is a reduction in the premium rate. Insurers can provide this lower rate because of the volume of business the group offers and because of lower commissions paid to agents for such sales.

- Employers provide the convenience of paying premiums through payroll deductions. It must again be emphasized that this is not an instance of group insurance—it is an arrangement of convenience by which the policyholder pays the employer, who then passes the money along to the insurer. In the case of an association, members may pay premiums to a designated person who then pays the insurer.

Thus, franchise plans are a way of providing some of the advantages of group insurance to those who do not have access to group insurance itself. People in this category include employees of smaller firms, members of associations, and members of groups that do not meet the legal definition of a group eligible for group insurance under state insurance laws. Franchise plans also have advantages for the insurer—they are an effective and economical way to market and service individual insurance policies for people in these circumstances. And for the employer, they are a way to attract and retain employees by giving them the opportunity of acquiring health insurance, without the employer contributing to the cost.

Insurers have developed new products, billing procedures, and underwriting practices to meet the needs of this market. Products include hospital and surgical expense insurance, major medical insurance, disability income insurance, and various supplemental coverages. Insurers also sell supplemental policies through franchise plans in cases where an employer provides basic group health insurance but employees want to add to their coverage.

Policies sold in this way usually offer coverage to dependents, except in the case of disability income insurance. These policies may be renewable at the option of the insurer or may be of a guaranteed renewable type. Typically the insured may not continue coverage when she leaves the group, but very often she has the opportunity to convert to a similar policy offered by the insurer.

Internet

Many insurance companies now maintain Internet sites that permit direct contact with the public. These sites provide product information, rate quotes, and in some cases company comparisons. As with other mass marketing techniques, the actual selling is usually done by phone or by an agent in person, but sales and payment of initial premiums over the Internet is possible and will likely become common.

Product Research and Development

To develop ideas for new products and improvements in existing products, and to ensure that these innovations meet real consumer needs and support corporate goals, insurers undertake research and development (R&D) activities. R&D functions may be carried out by an R&D department (sometimes called the product management department) or by a specially appointed ad hoc committee. In either case, experts from various departments of the company are usually consulted.

Most insurers define their overall goals and strategy in developing new products in a **product development statement**. This statement clarifies the financial objectives of product development efforts, the customers the insurer seeks to target, and the degree of financial risk the company is willing to undertake. Any new product must be compatible with the product development statement.

The development process for a new product (or an improvement in an existing product) has seven stages. At the end of each stage, project managers decide whether the development project should proceed to the next stage. This decision is based on compatibility with the insurer's product development statement as well as other factors such as resources available for the project and projections of profits from it.

Stage One: Idea Generation

An idea for a new product is proposed. The idea could be suggested by field sales personnel, home office staff, or senior management, based on their perceptions of consumer needs.

Stage Two: Market Research

Research is undertaken to determine if there is really a need for the proposed product (market needs studies) and to what extent competitors are already meeting this need (competition and market penetration studies). A detailed analysis of sales results may be made to help obtain this information. Studies may also be done to determine the best location for sales offices.

Stage Three: Product Outline

A product outline is developed. It clarifies:

- who the product is intended for—that is, the target market (for example, a group size and type, a geographic area, an industry, a socioeconomic group, etc.);
- what characteristics differentiate the product from others;

- how much developing the product will cost (a preliminary estimate); and
- what benefits will be derived from developing the product.

Stage Four: Market Analysis

A market analysis examines the proposed product in terms of the following questions:

- Is the product compatible with the insurer's product development statement? (That is, does it match the insurer's overall goals in terms of financial objectives, acceptable financial risk, and targeted markets?)
- What expertise and ability will be required to develop the product?
- Will the product work well with the other products and services the insurer already sells in the market it services?
- Can the insurer's current distribution and administration systems handle the product?
- How will sale of the product be influenced by the other "players in the game" (consumers, providers of health care, the government, and competitors)?

Stage Five: Product Design and Development

Product design and development involves:

- creating the contract for the product and filing it with state insurance departments;
- developing premium rates and commission schedules;
- setting underwriting limits, requirements, and guidelines, and creating underwriting manuals;
- developing sales training programs and materials, including agent training materials, sales manuals, sales presentations, and competitive comparisons;
- creating sales presentation materials, such as brochures, mailers, flip charts, and (in the case of larger insurers) films, videotapes, and audio recordings; and
- modifying data processing systems and administrative processes (proposing, rating, issuing, billing, accounting, benefits processing, and ongoing administrative maintenance).

Stage Six: Product Introduction

The sales department (with the help of any supporting departments) presents the product to prospects and begins selling.

Stage Seven: Sales Monitoring and Review

After the new product has been introduced and has become a part of the company's product line, it is monitored and reviewed to determine how it is performing. This includes analysis of sales results, analysis of a number of quotes, and input from the insurer's sales staff and agents.

Trends in the Marketing of Health Insurance Products

- The health care field continues to evolve rapidly. Insurers will have to continue to develop innovative products to meet new needs, explore new markets, and develop new or modify existing distribution systems.
- Some recent federal and state laws require that certain coverages provide certain benefits. These are known as **mandated benefits**. This situation has created a challenge to insurers to develop products that provide the required benefits while remaining affordable and profitable.
- The proliferation of e-commerce has become a competitive issue for all insurers. Internet sales and proposals are only the beginning of a new era of rapidly developing technological marketing strategies.
- The **Financial Services Modernization Act of 1999** removes Depression-era barriers between banking, securities, and insurance, paving the way for greater marketing of insurance through financial holding companies. The law has obvious potential for changing the insurance marketplace, but at this early date the impact it will have remains unclear. Health insurance is not likely to be in the forefront of those changes, although specialty coverages such as long-term care insurance may lend themselves to the markets that financial services companies want to reach.

Summary

The concept of marketing has broadened in recent years. It is now understood to mean all activities of a company that affect, directly or indirectly, new sales or the continuance of old business. Consequently, personnel in many departments are involved, not just sales people and product developers. However, the core activities of marketing remain identifying a market, evaluating the needs of that market, developing products to meet those needs, and promoting and distributing those products. The success and growth of an insurance company depends both on the success of its marketing personnel in performing core marketing activities and on the degree to which all personnel of the company see the ultimate purpose of their work as the attraction and retention of business.

15 UNDERWRITING OF GROUP HEALTH INSURANCE

- **Principles of Group Underwriting**

- **The Group Underwriting Process**

- **Large Groups and Small Groups**

- **Declining to Offer Coverage**

- **Projecting Claims: Adjusting Averages for Group Characteristics**

- **Projecting Claims: Examining a Group's Claims Experience**

- **Examining the Provisions of an Existing Plan**

- **Setting Premium Rates for an Existing Plan**

- **Underwriting and Managed Care**

- **Information Sources for Group Underwriting**

Introduction

Underwriting is the process by which an insurer determines whether and on what terms it will offer coverage to an applicant. This chapter examines the underwriting of group health insurance, including the work underwriters do, the factors they consider, and the information they use. The following chapter will discuss underwriting of individual health insurance.

Both chapters focus on full-time underwriters working in an insurer's home office, but the information is broadly applicable to the underwriting work sometimes done by agents and field sales personnel. Likewise, while the chapters mostly address medical expense and disability income insurance, the principles apply to underwriting for all health insurance coverages.

Principles of Group Underwriting

Prediction of Claims

As stated above, underwriting is the process of deciding whether and on what terms to offer coverage. The underwriter first ascertains if there is any reason the insurer should not offer coverage in the case under consideration. If it is decided to offer coverage, she then determines what the terms of that coverage should be. "Terms" in this context means the benefits that the insurer will provide, the premiums that the policyholder will pay, and other provisions of the contract.

In group insurance (unlike individual insurance), an offer is almost always made, for reasons that will be explained below. Therefore, the focus of group underwriting is deciding on the terms of the offer. On what basis is this decision made? The underwriter must write a policy with benefits, premium rates, and other provisions such that the insurer will earn enough money from premiums to pay the claims of group members and also make a reasonable profit (or in the case of mutual insurers, an allowance for addition to surplus). In order to write such a policy, the underwriter must know at least roughly what the level of claims will be. Therefore, the essence of underwriting is the prediction of claims.

The group underwriter tries to predict how many claims the members of the group will make, what the amounts of those claims will be, and thus how much the insurer will pay in claims if it provides coverage. Based on that projection of claims, the underwriter then determines what the terms of coverage should be—that is, she decides two things: how much the insurer must charge in premiums in order to earn enough to cover claims and make a profit, and what benefit provisions must be written into the policy to ensure that claims do not go above the predicted level.

Statistical Averages

How are predictions of claims made? As explained in the first chapter of this book, although no one can predict whether a certain individual will become ill, we can predict with a fair degree of accuracy the incidence of illness in a group. We do this by looking at the average experience of groups in the past and assuming that future experience will be similar. For example, an underwriter considering insuring a group of 300 people can find out the average level of claims for groups of that size and can assume with a high degree of probability that the group she is considering will have a roughly similar level of claims.

This simple example shows how underwriting works in principle. In fact, underwriting is much more sophisticated. For example, an underwriter does not usually make predictions of claims based solely on the number of people in the group.

She also factors in the group's characteristics. For instance, groups with many older members will have a higher level of health insurance claims than groups with mostly young members. If an underwriter knows the average age of the members of a group, she refers to the claims experience of other groups with the same average age and uses this information to make her prediction even more reliable. Other general characteristics of the group, such as the proportion of men and women, can be used in the same way.

Actual Claims Experience

In most instances, the group the underwriter is considering is not seeking insurance for the first time. Rather, the group has had coverage from another insurer and wants to change insurers. In this case, the underwriter can look at the claims made by the group while the other insurer's coverage was in effect. That is, the underwriter can base her prediction not only on average claims for other groups of similar size and characteristics, but also on the actual claims of this particular group, working on the assumption that the group's past experience will be repeated in the future.

Adverse Selection

In some group plans, eligible members have the option of having coverage (and paying premiums) or not. In such cases, those members who are more likely to become ill, either because they are older or because they are less healthy than average, are more likely to choose coverage. This phenomenon is known as adverse selection. (It was mentioned previously in relation to flexible benefits plans.) If adverse selection occurs, the covered group is not truly average, but rather has a higher level of claims than an average group. Consequently, underwriters' predictions of claims, if they are based on statistical averages, will be lower than actual claims, and premiums, since they are based on those predictions, may be too low to pay for claims. For this reason, one of the responsibilities of underwriters is to be alert to indications of adverse selection.

Profitability vs. Competitiveness

There is another consideration in underwriting. As has been explained, the underwriter must set terms that enable the insurer to realize a profit. At the same time, however, the underwriter must strive to offer terms that are attractive to the prospect, so that the prospect will choose the insurer's offer over another. In other words, in setting the terms of an offer, the underwriter must balance profitability and competitiveness. This competition among insurers works to make terms more favorable to policyholders.

The Group Underwriting Process

The process of underwriting an application for group health insurance is based on the principles explained above and includes the steps outlined below. Most insurers issue **underwriting manuals** that establish procedures and standards for these steps.

Deciding Whether to Offer Coverage

As noted above, in theory the first decision an underwriter makes is whether or not to offer coverage, but in practice a group underwriter will almost always make an offer. In the case of small groups, regulations do not usually allow the insurer to decline to offer coverage. For large groups, an insurer is free to decline but rarely does so, as almost all large groups are acceptable risks. However, there are a few circumstances in which large groups are not acceptable and the insurer will decline to offer coverage. These will be explained later in the chapter.

Making Assumptions about Benefits

If, as is usual, an underwriter decides to offer coverage to a group, he must of course predict the claims of the group. But he cannot predict the number and amounts of claims that a group will make without first making assumptions about what kind of claims group members will have the right to make—that is, what benefits members will be eligible for under the contract. Thus, in order to project claims, the underwriter assumes a tentative set of benefit provisions. In the case of a new group, he bases his assumptions on the set of benefits requested by the group. In the much more common case of an existing group, the underwriter assumes a continuation of existing benefits, modified to take into account any changes in benefits requested by the group. In both cases, modifications may be necessary to reflect the benefits that the new insurer is willing to provide. (An insurer's underwriting manuals usually establish minimum and maximum benefits acceptable to the insurer.)

Projecting Claims and Other Insurer Expenses

Once the underwriter has decided what benefits he will assume for the group, he can predict claims and the other expenses that will be incurred by the insurer in providing those benefits. As explained above, projections of claims may be based on the actual claims experience of the group, statistical averages for similar groups, or both.

- If statistical averages are used, the underwriter must ascertain the characteristics of the group (average age, gender distribution, etc.) and apply this information to statistical knowledge. Underwriting manuals usually contain standard projections of claims and adjustments for group characteristics.
- If information on the group's actual claims experience is used, the underwriter must determine the credibility of the information and use it to accurately predict future claims.

In projecting claims, the underwriter must carefully examine all information on the group to determine if the group diverges from the norm in any way that would warrant making an exception to the insurer's standard procedures. This includes probing for any indications of adverse selection. Finally, the underwriter must calculate expenses not related to claims, such as the administrative costs of providing coverage.

Making Final Decisions on Terms

Once cost projections are completed, the underwriter must recommend terms (premiums charged, benefits provided, and other provisions of the contract). Premium rates, like claims projections, are based on statistical averages, actual experience of the group, or both. When they are based on statistics, insurer **rating manuals** provide standard rates and adjustments for group characteristics. (Rates are also subject to state laws and regulations.)

Sometimes the benefit provisions requested by a group and assumed by the underwriter in predicting claims result in high claims projections and consequently unacceptably high premium rates. In such cases, the underwriter may suggest that the benefit provisions be modified in the final contract so that premiums can be kept at an affordable level.

Underwriting the Insurer's Existing Groups

Underwriters are also involved in making decisions on renewals and revisions of an insurer's existing health insurance plans. When a plan comes up for renewal, underwriters analyze the claims and other expenses of the plan to determine whether modifications in terms should be made and what they should be. Likewise, if a revision in the provisions of a plan is proposed, underwriters must do studies to determine what the impact of the suggested changes will be.

In this section a basic outline of the steps of the underwriting process has been given. The remainder of the chapter will cover in greater detail the activities that make up these steps.

Large Groups and Small Groups

Underwriting differs for large and small groups. Although there is some variation, in general for underwriting purposes groups with 2–50 insureds are considered small, and those with more than 50 insureds are considered large. This is the division adopted by the Health Insurance Portability and Accountability Act of 1996 (HIPAA). It should be noted that large and small groups are defined differently for sales and marketing. (See Chapter 14.)

Actual Claims Experience or Statistical Averages?

It was explained at the beginning of this chapter that the projection of claims may be based on the actual claims experience of the group being considered or on statistical averages adjusted for the characteristics of the group. We will now ask the question: Which method should be used in a given case? Obviously, if a group is newly formed and has no claims experience, averages will have to be used. But for a group that has already been insured, a choice must be made.

In making this choice, two principles must be taken into account. First, other things being equal, actual experience is a better predictor than statistical averages. That is, the actual behavior of a group is probably a better indication of its future behavior than the behavior of other groups of the same size and same general characteristics. On the other hand, in all statistical prediction, the larger the body of data that the prediction is based on, the more accurate the prediction will be. (For example, in political polling a sample of 1,000 people is usually more accurate than a sample of 100.)

If a small group is being underwritten, these two principles conflict. The actual claims experience of the group may be useful, but because it is such a small statistical sample, it may not be as accurate a predictor as the average experience of many other groups.

If a large group is being underwritten, there is no conflict between the two principles. The group has enough members to make a statistically reliable sample, and so actual claims experience of the group will predict more accurately than statistical studies.

To better understand this, consider the following example: it would not be unusual for a group of 10 people to go an entire year with no one having a serious illness. It would also not be unusual for one of these 10 people to require very expensive medical treatment in the following year. If these 10 people alone made up an insured group, the claims for that group would be very low in the first year and very high in the second year, and a prediction of claims for the second year based on the experience of the first year would be very inaccurate. On the other hand, if the same 10 people were members of an insured group of 1,000, in both years their unusual experience would be counterbalanced by the more typical experience of a large number of other people, and the level of claims for the whole group would be about the same both years. A claims projection for the second year based on the experience of all 1,000 people in the first year would be quite accurate.

Thus, for large groups the level of claims is usually roughly the same every year, and so the actual claims experience of a large group can be used to project future claims of that group. For small groups, on the other hand, the level of claims fluctuates greatly from year to year, and so underwriters cannot rely too much on actual experience.

Projections for small groups are not as accurate as for large groups. This is because claims projections for large groups are based on a large body of actual claims data for the group being considered (that is, the data is both specific to the group in question and large enough to be statistically reliable), while projections for small groups are based largely on general averages. In underwriting their existing groups (for renewals and revisions), most insurers address this problem by "pooling the experience" of their small groups. This means that although the groups in fact remain separate, for statistical purposes they are combined into one large **experience pool**, and claims projections are made for that pool. Some insurers, rather than create a single large group, combine categories of small groups into several larger experience pools. This gives underwriters of small groups one of the advantages of large group underwriting—the ability to base claims projections on a large body of actual claims experience.

While claims projections for large groups are usually more accurate, the degree of accuracy required for such groups is much greater. An inaccurate claims projection for a large group obviously has a much greater impact on an insurer's overall finances than an equally inaccurate projection for a small group. For example, a small group with a level of claims 10 to 20 percent higher than projected would not cause a major financial loss, but a large group with a similar deviation from projections could produce a loss running into hundreds of thousands of dollars— a significant amount for even the largest of insurers.

Premium Rates

Since a group's premium rate is based largely on the expected level of claims of the group, the setting of rates by underwriters follows the same pattern as the projection of claims. For small groups, underwriters use averages. (Specifically, as noted earlier, they use standard rates and adjustments for group characteristics from the insurer's rating manual; these rates and adjustments are based on statistical averages of claims.) For very large groups, rates are based entirely on the actual claims experience of the group. For some medium-size groups, a mixed approach may be used—standard rates are used but with an adjustment for actual claims experience.

A group's level of claims may sometimes turn out to be much lower than projected. In such cases, the insurer may reduce the group's rates or even give an experience refund if a provision for this is included in the contract.

Adverse Selection

Adverse selection can occur in groups of any size, but it is a particular concern with small groups. Consider the following situation: The owner of a business does not provide health insurance to his employees. Then, one of his family members contracts an illness that will require expensive medical treatment. At that point the businessman decides to get group coverage for his employees, which will also cover himself and his dependents. In a large group, the claims of the businessman's dependent would not have a great impact on overall claims levels. In a small group, on the other hand, because there are many fewer members to counterbalance the experience of one individual, a single person with a serious illness can cause a significant increase in claims.

Many insurers have addressed the problem of adverse selection in small groups by excluding preexisting conditions or by requiring evidence of the insurability of the individual members of the group and sometimes their dependents. However, HIPAA and many state laws limit the use of preexisting condition exclusions (as explained in Chapter Three) and prohibit the exclusion from coverage of individual employees based on their health status.

Small Group Regulations

In addition, HIPAA and the **small group market reforms** enacted by many states in the early 1990s require that insurers serving the small group market accept any small group that applies and that is eligible under the law. This is known as **guaranteed issue**. Therefore, as noted above, underwriting for small groups under guaranteed issue conditions does not include deciding whether or not to offer coverage to the group, since the insurer does not have this choice. In this situation underwriting includes only ascertaining whether the group is eligible and determining the terms that will be offered to the group.

Administrative Costs and Benefits

Small groups have higher administrative costs per insured person than large groups. In an effort to keep administrative costs down, insurers usually try to keep plans for small groups simple and limit benefit variations.

Declining to Offer Coverage

Sometimes, although rarely, an underwriter will recommend that the insurer not offer coverage to a group, typically for one of the reasons listed below. (It should be remembered that regulations usually prohibit an insurer from refusing coverage to a small group.)

Low Participation

If only a small proportion of the eligible members of a group enroll in a plan, the enrolled group will have a much larger than average number of individuals with health problems. In other words, adverse selection will occur.

Fictitious Groups

A fictitious group is a group created solely for the purpose of obtaining insurance for its members. Underwriting is based on the assumption that any group being considered is a random sample of people and that therefore the group includes an average mix of healthy and less healthy individuals. For groups that form for a reason other than insurance (such as employment), this is very likely the case. On the other hand, a group formed to obtain insurance for its members is almost certainly made up of people who are very likely to incur medical expenses. This is another example of adverse selection.

Policyholder Administration

If a policyholder does not properly administer a group plan (for example, if it enrolls employees late or does not properly record terminations), the insurer can face frequent and time-consuming problems. Therefore, if the underwriter believes that the policyholder is not able to adequately administer the plan, she will recommend that the insurer decline to offer coverage.

Expected Persistency

An insurer incurs substantial expenses when it first insures a group. These are referred to as **acquisition expenses**, and include the costs of sales activities, underwriting, and contract issuance. The underwriter wants to be reasonably sure that, barring special circumstances, a new group will stay with the insurer for a reasonable period (certainly not less than three years) so that these expenses can be recovered. The underwriter therefore usually declines to offer coverage to temporary businesses (such as those created for a specific limited project) or businesses in financial difficulties.

Projecting Claims: Adjusting Averages for Group Characteristics

As explained earlier, claims projections and premium rates for small and medium-size groups are based on standard averages adjusted for general characteristics of the group. We will now look in more detail at some of those characteristics, including age, gender, dependent participation, occupation or type of business, income, and geographical location. (Note that when claims projections and rates for a group are based on the group's experience rather than on averages, as with most large groups, no such adjustment is made, since the actual claims experience of the group already reflects the impact of these characteristics.)

Age

Older people make more medical expense and disability income claims than younger people. Adjustments are based on the average age of the group.

Gender

Women generally make more health insurance claims than men, and have a 25 percent greater incidence of disabilities. Men's claims are greater only for accidental death and dismemberment insurance. Adjustments are based on the proportion of men and women in the group.

Dependent Participation

Most groups include dependents. The proportion of a group's insureds who are dependents affects claims levels, since dependents are children and spouses, and age and gender affect claims. In recent years the traditional proportions of dependents have changed because of the increase in single-parent households and the decrease in the average number of children per family. The increase in working women has also had an impact, as dependent participation may be low if many employees have spouses with coverage from their own employers. This is especially likely if an employee group has a high proportion of married women, whose husbands' insurance often covers the children.

Type of Business

Generally, health insurance does not provide benefits for illnesses and accidents resulting directly from a person's employment. Such benefits are provided by each state's workers' compensation program. However, group health coverage usually does cover ailments that result indirectly from work activities or the physical environment of the workplace, and conditions likely to indirectly cause health problems are more common in some kinds of businesses than in others. For example, employees working in a very hot area such as a foundry are more susceptible to respiratory ailments, and employees who must sit for long periods of time are more likely to have back problems. In the underwriting of employee groups, adjustments must be made to reflect the different claims levels of different kinds of business.

In other cases, the environment or work activities typical of a certain kind of business do not indirectly cause health conditions, but nonetheless workers in that field are on average less healthy. For example, restaurants and parking garages generally pay low wages and so tend to attract workers who cannot meet the health standards of more selective employers. Adjustments must be made for these businesses as well.

Income

People with higher-than-average incomes generally get more frequent and higher-priced medical care, so a group with a disproportionate number of high-income individuals will have high claims. On the other hand, low-paying jobs are more likely to involve working conditions that indirectly cause health problems, so groups with a large proportion of low-income workers may also have high claims.

Geography

Although the geographical location of a group does not generally significantly affect the number of claims made, it does affect the cost of those claims. Charges for medical care vary widely by geographic area. Hospitals in the Southeast United States charge less on average than those in the Northeast, and charges in urban areas are generally higher than in rural areas.

Group Characteristics as Indicators of Problems

The characteristics of groups must be examined not only because they have an impact on the level of claims, but also because unusual characteristics can signal potential problems. For example, a group might have a high average age because the business hires very few new employees, which might be an indication of financial difficulties. On the other hand, a very young group could indicate high turnover, which would entail high administrative costs for the insurer. High turnover can also result in a rapid and significant change in the characteristics of the group, possibly making rates inadequate.

Projecting Claims: Examining a Group's Claims Experience

When an insurer is considering taking over an existing plan, the group already has claims experience. For large groups, underwriting will be based on this experience. For small groups, underwriting will be based largely on statistical averages, but for both large and small groups, the underwriter should examine claims data for any indications of problems. For example, the underwriter should try to determine the reason the group is seeking to change insurers. Such a change is not unusual, and the reason may be to get a better rate, better service, or more managed care options. However, the underwriter would be unwise to ignore the possibility that the transfer is being sought because the group's present insurer has or is about to raise rates as a result of very high claims.

If the underwriting of a group is to be based on past claims data, the underwriter must first examine the data to determine that they are complete, accurate, and reliable. In judging the **reliability of data** (that is, how accurately the data will predict future claims), the underwriter considers these questions:

- Is the group large enough for the data to be reliable? In other words, is the group large enough that the level of claims is usually about the same every year, or is it so small that claims may fluctuate widely from year to year?
- Does the claims data cover a sufficient length of time to be reliable? Even large groups experience some year-to-year fluctuations, and claims data can be abnormally high or low in any given year. If data from several years are available, the typical annual amount of claims will be much clearer.

In addition, when a group has a high level of claims, the underwriter must examine the claims to determine if this high level is a reliable predictor of future claims, that is, if it is likely to continue. If the high level is the result of many small claims, it is probably the true level of claims of the group and will likely continue. However, if it is the result of a few very large claims, such claims may represent unusual cases that may or may not recur or continue. For example, a very large claim could be for an unusual accident that probably will not recur. Or it could be for a catastrophic illness for which no more claims will be made because the victim has died. On the other hand, a large claim could be for a chronic condition that will continue indefinitely. If a large claim is not considered likely to continue or recur, the underwriter may disregard a substantial part of that claim in projecting future claims. If, on the other hand, the claim is considered likely to continue or recur, it must be included in the underwriter's calculations.

The completeness, accuracy, and reliability of past claims data are of particular concern for very large groups. This is because claims projections and premium rates for large groups are generally based solely on such data, and because the larger the group, the greater the financial impact on the insurer of an inaccurate projection of claims.

Because it involves the examination and analysis of claims data, the underwriting of an existing group requires more work than the underwriting of new groups. Underwriters must be given sufficient time to adequately review all information. It should also be kept in mind that evaluating claims experience is not an exact science and problems arise for which there are no clear-cut answers. Each underwriter makes decisions based on his own experience and the insurer's established procedures.

Examining the Provisions of an Existing Plan

When an insurer is considering taking over an existing plan, the provisions of the plan become a factor in underwriting. The underwriter must obtain as much information as possible about the previous plan; he usually prefers to review the contract, but a copy of the employee booklet or certificate of insurance will often suffice. The underwriter also tries to obtain information about the present insurer's actions on renewal of the plan. For example, the insurer may have proposed, as a condition of renewal, changes such as increased deductibles or additional limitations that were intended to solve specific claim problems.

The underwriter first ascertains if there are any provisions in the existing plan that differ significantly from the new insurer's standard contract. The underwriter studies these provisions to determine what impact they may have, and may or may not include them in the new plan. If changes are made, the insurer must make this clear to the policyholder.

The contract provisions that are most important in underwriting are those that deal with eligibility for coverage, minimum enrollment requirements, requirements for dependent participation, premium cost sharing, benefits, administration, and the handling of existing claims.

Eligibility for Coverage

All employees of a business may be eligible for coverage under one group health plan, or different classes of employees may be covered by different plans, or only certain classes may have any coverage. From the insurer's point of view, inclusion of all employees in one plan is the most desirable approach, since this creates a larger group. However, sometimes hourly-paid employees and salaried (professional and managerial) employees have different health plans. Often this is because the hourly workers' health plan is determined by collective bargaining between the employer and a union. A group made up of only salaried employees is not a problem provided it is sufficiently large. However, the underwriter must exercise caution if only executives and key personnel are to be covered by a plan. There is a great potential for adverse selection in this situation, as executives may request plan provisions with the intention of ensuring coverage for a specific health condition of one of the executives or a member of an executive's family.

While insurers prefer that all permanent full-time employees be covered by the same plan, they generally prefer that part-time, seasonal, and temporary employees be covered separately. This is because these employees have high turnover and consequently high administrative costs.

Minimum Enrollment Requirements

As noted in Chapter Nine, when employees have the option of enrolling in a coverage or not, there is usually a contract provision requiring that a minimum number or percentage of all employees enroll. This provision is necessary to avoid adverse selection. If only a small percentage of employees enroll, the enrolled group may have a larger than average number of individuals with health problems.

Requirements for Dependent Participation

Just as most group insurance contracts require that a minimum number of employees participate in a health plan, most also require that a certain percentage (typically 75 percent) of employees carry coverage for their dependents. However, a plan may not be able to require this percentage if many employees have spouses with coverage from their own employers. Where there is low dependent participation, insurers may make inquiries to determine if other coverage is in effect. If this is the case, the insurer may exclude dependents with other coverage in determining if requirements for dependent participation have been met. However, if only a few employees choose dependent coverage, the insurer runs the risk of adverse selection.

Premium Cost Sharing

The payment of premiums under a plan may be **noncontributory** (the employee contributes nothing because the employer pays all of the premium) or **contributory** (the employee pays a portion or all). From the insurer's point of view, payment on a noncontributory basis is preferable because it ensures participation of all employees, which has the following advantages:

- A larger group is created.
- There is no possibility of adverse selection (since employees do not choose to participate or not).
- Administration is simplified. (In contributory plans employees must enroll individually, and in some plans late entrants must submit evidence of insurability. These tasks are eliminated in noncontributory plans, where all employees are automatically enrolled.)

Some contributory plans are **fully contributory**, meaning the insureds pay all of the premium. These plans are also known as "employee-pay-all" or voluntary plans. Fully contributory payment has a number of disadvantages for an insurer:

- The insurer may not be able to offer a fully adequate plan, since the average employee may not be able to pay the full cost of such a plan.
- Due to the high cost to employees, participation may be low, meaning that the group may be small and adverse selection a potential problem.
- Since any increases in premium rates will be passed on in full to the employee, maintaining participation will be difficult.
- An employer's refusal to contribute financially may indicate a lack of interest in the plan that could result in poor administration and a lack of cooperation with the insurer.

For these reasons, most insurers only offer such coverages as long-term care insurance or voluntary accidental death and dismemberment insurance on a fully contributory basis. Even then, insurers usually insist on minimum participation requirements. In addition, fully contributory plans are not permitted by the laws of some states.

Benefits

The careful examination of an existing plan can reveal benefit provisions that might have resulted in high claims, causing the old insurer to require an increase in rates as a condition of renewal, which in turn might be the employer's reason for seeking to transfer coverage to a different insurer. If this is the case, the insurer must require modifications of these provisions or a premium rate sufficient to cover them.

If the group covered by the existing plan is large enough to warrant special plan design, the insurer may propose an expansion of benefits, provided the proposed premium rates will pay for these benefits and the insurer can administratively handle them.

The underwriter should pay particular attention to existing plans in which the benefits are either minimal or very liberal. Minimal benefits can be indicative of policyholder financial problems. In addition, if the benefits of a plan are inadequate, many employees will seek additional coverage by purchasing individual policies, which may result in overinsurance. Overinsurance was discussed in the section on coordination of benefits (COB) in Chapter Eight. It occurs when one expense is covered by more than one insurance policy, making it possible for the insured to receive more in benefits than his actual losses. Since the COB provision in most group plans does not coordinate benefits with individual policies, this kind of overinsurance is difficult to prevent or even detect.

Liberal plans have different potential problems. If they are contributory, the contribution required from the employee is often large, leading to low participation, a small group, and possible adverse selection. Low-income employees will be especially likely to choose not to participate, giving the group a high average income. In a very small group, the choice of generous benefits may be motivated by the desire to provide broad coverage for an existing condition of a key employee.

Administration

An insurance contract stipulates the administrative responsibilities of the policyholder and the insurer. When a plan is transferred, the policyholder usually expects that this division of responsibilities will remain roughly the same. The policyholder also usually expects procedures to remain the same and existing records to be carried over. These expectations may conflict with the standard operations and procedures of the insurer. The underwriter must determine what the administrative expectations of the policyholder are so that she can determine if the insurer will be able to meet them or if modifications will have to be made. Some of the most important potential problems can be identified by asking the following questions:

- Will the insurer's standard billing and claims procedures be acceptable to the policyholder?
- Will the policyholder accept **self-billing,** that is, will the policyholder take responsibility for the billing of individual members, or must the insurer bill individuals?
- If the employer has multiple locations, will separate record keeping, billing, and claim processing be required for each location?

If any special administrative provisions are made to accommodate the policyholder, the underwriter must determine their cost and adjust premiums accordingly.

Existing Claims

The underwriter must take into account how existing claims will be handled if an existing plan is transferred. Some states have **"no loss-no gain"** regulations for group insurance. These regulations usually stipulate that no group member shall lose benefit payments for an existing health condition when the group's plan is transferred. They also usually prohibit the new insurer from applying preexisting condition limitations to individuals who are already members of the existing plan.

In states without "no loss-no gain" regulations, the employer may ask the new insurer to comply with their spirit anyway—that is, to cover existing health conditions and waive preexisting condition limitations for present members. HIPAA also restricts exclusions of preexisting conditions when a group plan is transferred. (See Chapter Three.)

Some group insurance policies stipulate that if insureds are receiving benefits for some conditions (such as total disability) when the contract is terminated, they will continue to receive benefits for some period of time after termination. This is known as **extended benefits**. Underwriters should be aware of any such provisions in the existing contract so that the new insurer does not provide duplicate benefits.

Setting Premium Rates for an Existing Plan

After examining an existing group's claim experience and the provisions of the existing contract, an underwriter recommends a proposed plan design. This must include rates. Generally, an insurer sets rates for an existing large group by proceeding as if it already provided coverage to the group and was considering renewing the policy. That is, the insurer determines what the renewal rate would be for one of its groups with the same claims experience and the same benefits. For small groups standard rates from rating manuals are used.

Underwriting and Managed Care

A growing number of employers are transferring their group plans in order to maximize employee utilization of managed care. In addition, insurers offering to take over an existing plan or renewing one of their own plans often recommend a shift to managed care. This situation has created significant underwriting complexities and challenges. If a plan is moving to managed care, the underwriter must estimate savings in claims and adjust premiums accordingly. If an insurer is replacing a plan's HMO or PPO with another, underwriting is particularly complex. The underwriter must take into account the following:

- the proportion of plan members who participate in managed care;
- the portion of claims attributable to the managed care options of the plan;
- trends in the above two areas;
- the discounts and savings attributable to managed care under the existing HMO and/or PPO; and
- the discounts and savings projected under the new HMO and/or PPO.

Information Sources for Group Underwriting

The Request for Proposals (RFP)

A request for proposals (RFP), as explained in the section on the group sales process, is a document issued by an employer that notifies insurers that the employer is seeking coverage and invites them to propose an insurance plan. The RFP and accompanying forms provide information useful in underwriting, including:

- the group's claim history;
- employee data, such as the number of employees participating, the number eligible, and whether there are any excluded classes;
- the employer's prior insurance history, which helps the underwriter determine whether the employer is likely to continue with the insurer; and
- the plan provisions desired or required by the group.

Enrollment Cards

Enrollment cards usually provide information about age, gender, earnings, dependents, and occupation.

Inspection Reports

Insurers sometimes use commercial investigating companies to obtain underwriting information about smaller groups. Representatives of these companies visit the business, report on any adverse working conditions, and help verify the eligibility information supplied by the employer in the RFP.

Federal Disclosure Reports

Employers with 100 or more insured employees are required under the **Employee Retirement Income Security Act (ERISA)** to distribute annual health plan experience reports to their employees and to file similar information with the U.S. Department of Labor. Underwriters often secure copies of these reports to verify the experience information supplied by the applicant.

Agents and Brokers

For new groups, insurers usually require the agent or broker to get detailed information from the policyholder about past experience, benefits, and rates and to pass it on to the insurer's group representative or home office.

Group Representatives

The insurer's group representative often visits the employer's premises to discuss the plan, and so may be able to give the underwriter firsthand information about the employer and employees.

Summary

Insurance companies must predict the amount of claims they will have to pay so that they can charge enough in premiums to pay those claims and make a profit. The projection of claims is the essence of underwriting. The claims projection for a group may be based on the experience of other groups with similar characteristics, or it may be based on the past claims of the group being considered. Based on the projected level of claims, the underwriter makes recommendations on what benefits can be provided and what premiums must be charged to cover the cost of claims. Underwriters' projections must not be too high, or premiums will be too high and the company will lose business to competitors. On the other hand, if projections are too low, premiums will not be sufficient to meet costs and the company will lose money. Thus the role of the underwriter is vital to a company's success and survival.

16 UNDERWRITING OF INDIVIDUAL HEALTH INSURANCE

- *Principles of Individual Underwriting*
- *Adjusting for General Characteristics*

- *Analyzing Information on the Individual*
- *The Individual Underwriting Process*

Introduction

Underwriting individual health insurance is similar in many ways to group underwriting. Both are based on the same principles and involve many of the same activities. However, there are important differences. Underwriters of individual policies often decline to offer coverage, which group underwriters rarely do and in some cases are not allowed to do. In addition, individual underwriters concern themselves with the health, occupation, and financial status of individuals, whereas group underwriters rely solely on group averages. Finally, because of this different focus, individual and group underwriters use different sources of information.

Principles of Individual Underwriting

In group insurance, it is usually assumed that, barring special circumstances, an offer of coverage will be made, and the underwriting process focuses on setting terms. In individual insurance, on the other hand, it is not assumed that coverage will be offered, and the decision to do so is an important part of underwriting. However, in both cases the fundamental purpose of underwriting is the same—the underwriter seeks to ensure that, for any coverage the insurer provides, the level of claims will not be higher than the premiums received. Therefore, the essence of individual underwriting, as for group underwriting, is the projection of claims.

How do we project claims for an individual? As in group underwriting, we rely on averages. We look at the past experience of many people, note how often they have become ill or injured over a certain period of time, and use this information to calculate how often, on average, any person will become ill or injured.

Of course, in order to illustrate a principle, we have greatly simplified things. Like group underwriting, individual underwriting is in practice much more complex. For example, like the group underwriter, the individual underwriter can make claims projections more accurate by basing them not on averages of all people, but on averages of people with the same general characteristics (age, gender, etc.) as the person being underwritten.

Individual underwriters also take a further step that is not usually a part of group underwriting. They examine each individual to determine whether for some reason she is significantly more likely than the average person to make claims. For example, if a person already suffers from severe asthma, claims for that condition are virtually a certainty. Or if a person has a history of heart attacks, another attack is much more likely for him than for the average person.

Why do individual underwriters take this additional step? Why don't they simply accept all applicants on the assumption that some people will be less healthy than others but that the claims of the many individuals they insure will balance out? The answer is adverse selection. In a preexisting group, such as all the employees of a business, the insurer can be reasonably sure that there is an average mix of people who are more healthy and people who are less healthy. This is not the case for a random group of individual policyholders. Many people seek individual health insurance because they have a particular problem or are much more likely than average to become ill. If an insurer accepted all such people, claims would be much higher than premiums. Consequently, underwriters of individual policies try to identify applicants likely to have a high level of claims and either decline to provide coverage, provide modified coverage, or adjust premiums.

Although insurers are usually allowed to decline to offer coverage to individuals, there are some restrictions. HIPAA guarantees availability of individual health insurance coverage without preexisting condition limitations to certain individuals who have lost group health coverage. Also, some state laws require guaranteed availability of individual insurance or limit rate differentials to different applicants.

Adjusting for General Characteristics

For the most part, general characteristics such as age and gender are taken into account in individual underwriting in the same way as in group underwriting. However, occupation and income are particularly important in underwriting individual policies for disability income and accidental death and dismemberment insurance.

Persons in professional occupations and those with high incomes have fewer disability claims and shorter periods of disability than average. Persons in occupations that require heavy manual labor or where there are accidental hazards have a greater number of disability claims and longer periods of disability than average. Based on these different levels of claims, insurers have established classes of occupations and use these classes to determine premium rates as well as the type and amount of coverage offered. Lower premiums, more liberal benefits, and higher maximum benefits are available to the classes with lower claims.

Occupation is not a major factor in underwriting individual medical expense insurance, and premiums do not usually vary by occupation. However, insurers may refuse to issue coverage to people in extremely hazardous occupations, such as professional rodeo riding or deep-sea diving, or they may issue them policies that exclude occupational injuries.

Analyzing Information on the Individual

The Applicant's Medical Condition and Medical History

The two most important factors in determining the probability of an individual having future medical problems are:

- the individual's **current physical condition**, and
- his **medical history**.

In considering these factors, individual underwriters ask two questions:

- Does the applicant's health history and current physical condition differ significantly from the average?
- What is the probable impact of current medical conditions and previous medical history on future claims?

Specifically, underwriters are concerned with the following:

- Does the applicant currently have a medical condition that will lead to claims? If so, what is the normal progression of the condition? (With some conditions, progression to the point of hospitalization or disability is possible.)
- Does the applicant have a condition that could lead to an additional illness or injury? For example, epilepsy increases the chances of an injury; obesity can lead to cardiovascular problems.
- Does the applicant have a condition (such as hypertension) that could prolong a disability from an unrelated cause?

- Did the applicant suffer in the past from an illness or injury that could recur or lead to complications? Most medical conditions do not recur and can be disregarded if recovery has been prompt and if there is no evidence of any residual impairment. Other conditions may recur or may have latent complications that do not emerge until much later.

The Applicant's Financial Status

The applicant's financial situation (her income, assets, and debts) is not a consideration in underwriting most coverages. However, it is important in underwriting individual disability income insurance. This is because the disability underwriter must set benefits at a level such that the insured's disability income is not a great deal less than her pre-disability income, but not so high that disability income is greater than or almost the same as pre-disability income. (If disability income is higher than or nearly equal to regular income, the insured would have no incentive to return to work.)

To set disability benefits at the appropriate level, the underwriter must consider the applicant's income, both earned and unearned (that is, from investments). He must also take into account the applicant's net worth. A high net worth is significant even if the applicant's assets are not producing substantial investment income at the time of underwriting. Assets could be shifted to income generating investments if the insured became disabled, and the resulting income combined with disability insurance benefits could lessen the insured's incentive to return to work.

The Individual Underwriting Process

Reviewing the Application

In underwriting individual health insurance, the underwriter first examines the application. The application is the main source of information for individual underwriting. The application includes:

- general information supplied by the applicant;
- statements made by the applicant about his current physical condition and medical history; and
- the applicant's signature, attesting that he has answered the questions truthfully and completely to the best of his knowledge and belief.

In practice, the applicant does not usually fill out the application himself. Rather, the agent asks the applicant questions and fills in the answers. However, the applicant must always sign the application to confirm the truth of the information in it.

The format of an application and the scope of its questions differ with different insurers and according to the application's use. Some applications are used for only one type of insurance and include only questions relevant to that coverage. Other applications are used for a variety of coverages and include a broader range of questions. (See Figure 16.1. for an example of an application.)

Reviewing the Agent's Statements

Most insurers provide space on the back of their applications for statements by agents. Information supplied by agents can include:

- how long and how well the agent has known the applicant;
- the applicant's approximate net worth, annual earned income, and income from sources other than employment;
- clarification of any information on the application that is questionable or unclear;
- any special circumstances or special problems not otherwise noted on the application; and
- any other information the agent has regarding the applicant that is not included on the application but that might be relevant to underwriting.

Obtaining Additional Information

After reviewing the application and the agent's statements, the underwriter may decide to provide the requested coverage, to offer modified coverage, or to reject the application. Or she many decide to try to obtain more information before making a decision. Additional information can include a medical or paramedical examination, an attending physician's statement, an inspection report from an independent investigator, documentation of the applicant's income, and information from industry-sponsored databases. An authorization form giving the underwriter permission to obtain required information from outside sources accompanies the application. It must be signed by the applicant.

Older people are more likely to have medical problems than younger people and are more likely to have problems not specifically asked about in the application. For this reason, the underwriting guidelines of most insurers call for more frequent use of medical examinations and physicians' statements for older applicants.

Medical examination. When an underwriter feels that he needs more information on an applicant's medical condition, whether because of age or for some other reason, he may require a medical examination. The examination provides information regarding height and weight, pulse, blood pressure, and other findings. The examining physician supplies this information on a form provided by the insurer. The applicant fills out the nonmedical sections of this form and both physician and applicant sign it.

FIGURE 16.1

Sample Application for Individual Life and Medical Expense Insurance

A. Applicant Information

Applicant's Name (Please Print) (First) (Middle) (Last)	Birthdate Mo. Day Year	Sex ☐ Male ☐ Female	Social Security Number

Street Address or P.O. Box	County you live in:	Are you a U.S. Citizen? ☐ Yes ☐ No

City State Zip Code	Telephone no. where we can reach you during the day Area Code( )

Applicant's Occupation/Nature of Business (if retired, nature of former business)

Are you currently covered by an employer sponsored group medical plan? ☐ Yes ☐ No

If yes, please indicate: Plan Number _____ Date Coverage to Cease _____

Carrier _____ Reason for Termination _____

B. Plan Information

Effective Date:

☐ I request insurance effective the 1st of the month following Home Office approval

OR

☐ I request insurance effective the 1st day of (month) _____ , 19 _____ . *

* *I understand I will be liable for premium from this date and the date cannot be changed even if notice of approval is not received by rhe until a later date.*

Applicant's Initials _____

Plan Options:	Optional Benefits:
Deductible $ _____	
☐ 80/20 ▬▬ ☐ 80/20 PPO	☐ Yes ☐ No Premium Saver
☐ 50/50 ▬▬ PPO Name _____	☐ Yes ☐ No Freedom Option
☐ _____ PPO Number _____	☐ Yes ☐ No Supplemental Life

Beneficiary Name: (First) (Middle) (Last) (Relationship)	Maternity:
	☐ No *If no, complications only will be covered.*
Beneficiary changes are not effective until recorded in the Home Office. Unless written otherwise, if more than one beneficiary is named, proceeds will be payable in equal shares to surviving beneficiaries. If more space is needed, use a "Request for Change of Beneficiary" form.	☐ Yes *If yes, I realize this plan includes a six month waiting period that begins the date the female becomes insured or elects full maternity coverage, whichever is later. Benefits may vary by state.* Applicant's Initials _____

Special Instructions:

C. Dependent Information - *Complete this section only if applying for Dependent Coverage. If so, list full names of all dependents.*

Marital Status: ☐ Single ☐ Married	Names	Sex M/F	Birthdate Mo. Day Yr.	F-Time Student	Foster Child	Step Child	Lives in Your Home?
	Spouse			(X)	(X)	(X)	Yes? No?
If any dependent is not approved, do you still want coverage for those who are approved? ☐ Yes ☐ No	Children 1.						
Special Notes:	2.						
Foster and stepchildren eligibility is subject to Home Office approval. If applying for coverage for foster children, complete Foster Child Questionnaire, ▬▬	3.						
	4.						
Dependents age 19 or older, must meet student eligibility requirements.	5.						

To be completed by Soliciting Agent ▶	Signature of Soliciting Agent		Agent's Group Code	Agent's Social Security No.
	Agent Name (Please Print) Street City	State	Zip	

To be completed by Regional Office ▶	Regional Office Signature Date Signed	Regional Office Signature (For Affiliate Program) Date Signed	Rep Code Off Code

To be completed by Home Office ▶	Effective Date of Coverage

FIGURE 16.1

(*continued*)

D. Medical History for Applicant and Dependents - *Give full details to any questions answered "yes."*

	Yes No
1. Applicant's Height ____ ft. ____ in. Weight ____ lbs. Gain or loss of 10 lbs. in the last year? If "yes," explain. ____	☐ ☐
2. Applicant's tobacco use: ☐ current ☐ past ☐ never Date last used _____ (If "never," skip to question 3) **Type/Frequency:** ☐ cigarettes ____ pks/day ☐ cigars ____ day ☐ pipes ____ full/day	
3. Spouse's Height ____ ft. ____ in. Weight ____ lbs. Gain or loss of 10 lbs. in the last year? If "yes," explain.	☐ ☐
4. Spouse's tobacco use: ☐ current ☐ past ☐ never Date last used _____ (If "never," skip to question 5) **Type/Frequency:** ☐ cigarettes ____ pks/day ☐ cigars ____ day ☐ pipes ____ full/day	
5. Is anyone now planning, scheduled for, getting or thinking about getting medical treatment, psychotherapy, counseling, having surgery, or taking any medicine, drugs, pills, shots etc?	☐ ☐
6. Has anyone been told of a need to schedule any tests, treatment, surgery, biopsy, hospitalization, or specialist consultation?	☐ ☐
7. Is anyone pregnant, or has anyone (male or female) been evaluated for infertility in the last 5 years?	☐ ☐
8. Does anyone have any physical or mental birth defects, a developmental or learning disability, a behavior disorder or a physical or mental impairment?	☐ ☐
9. Has anyone had persistent, lingering or prolonged fevers, night sweats, fatigue/tiredness or weakness in the last 2 years?	☐ ☐
10. Has anyone been told by a doctor, counselor, therapist or other medical specialist of the need to reduce or discontinue the use of alcohol or drugs in the last 5 years?	☐ ☐

IN THE LAST 10 YEARS HAS ANYONE:	Yes No
11. had surgery?	☐ ☐
12. been hospitalized?	☐ ☐
13. been to or consulted a doctor, chiropractor, counselor, therapist or any medical, dental, or eye specialist or had blood tests other than for HIV infection, other medical tests or been referred to a medical specialist?	☐ ☐
14. been treated for the use of alcohol or drugs?	☐ ☐
15. had any back, neck or spinal problems, a joint or muscle disorder?	☐ ☐
16. had gallbladder problems, ulcers, chronic diarrhea, colitis, other digestive problems, hepatitis, cirrhosis or liver problems?	☐ ☐
17. had urinary problems, a disorder of the reproductive system, menstrual disorder, breast disorders, venereal disease or other infectious disease?	☐ ☐
18. had shortness of breath, chronic cough, bronchitis, tuberculosis, asthma, pneumonia, or other respiratory problems?	☐ ☐
19. been unconscious, or had epilepsy, seizures, convulsions or other neurological disorder?	☐ ☐
20. had depression, stress, anxiety or received any counseling, psychotherapy, or had a mental or nervous disorder?	☐ ☐
21. had cancer, tumors, cysts or growths of any kind or a skin disorder? Benign? ☐ Malignant? ☐	☐ ☐
22. had diabetes, gout, arthritis, thyroid disorder, or a disorder of the lymph nodes or lymph system?	☐ ☐
23. had any chest pain, heart trouble, heart attack, heart murmur, rapid, slow or irregular heart beat, high blood pressure, stroke or other circulatory problems?	☐ ☐
24. had an EKG or stress test (exercise EKG)? If "yes," describe the reason for the test and the results.	☐ ☐
25. been treated for or diagnosed as having HIV infection, AIDS, AIDS-related Complex (ARC), or any disease or disorder of the immune system?	☐ ☐

NOTE: If more space is needed below, please attach a sheet of paper with additional information with your signature and date.
If either question 10 or 14 was answered yes, describe the frequency, amount and type of alcohol or drug used now or in the past.

Question No.From Above	Name of Person	Nature of Illness / Injury, Symptoms, Treatment, Testing, Medical Attention, Diagnosis	Date of onset mo-day-yr	Duration	Results, Findings, Remaining Symptoms / Problems	Names and Addresses of Physicians or Hospitals

E. Statement of Understanding and Authorization

- ▇▇▇▇▇▇▇▇▇▇▇▇▇▇▇▇▇▇
- I authorize any medical practitioner, medically-related facility, insurance company or any other organization, institution or person to give ▇▇▇▇ representatives any information about me or any named dependents, including physical or mental history and drug or alcohol use.
- I represent all information, statements and answers recorded on this ▇▇▇▇▇▇ as well as any attachments to this enrollment form are full, correct, and true to the best of my knowledge. I agree that a photostat of this form is as valid as the original. I understand that omissions and/or misstatements regarding age or medical history, could cause an otherwise valid claim to be denied and/or cause the insurance, if issued, to be cancelled as if never effective.
- Applicants will be informed whether or not application has been approved within 60 days or be given the reason for delay.

- I understand no insurance will become effective (a) unless medical history is evaluated and satisfactory to ▇▇▇▇ and (b) for anyone while home or hospital confined on the effective date.
- I understand the Effective Date will be the date I selected subject to approval by the home office ▇▇▇▇. The effective date cannot be on or before the date the application is signed.
- I understand I will be liable for all premium due from the effective date I selected in Section B even if notice of approval is received by me after that date.
- I authorize premiums to be drawn from my account at a financial institution.
- I understand the premium charged and coverage issued will be those offered on the Effective Date.
- I understand an agent cannot guarantee coverage or revise rates, benefits or plan provisions without the written approval by an officer of

Signature of Applicant   Date Signed

Often an applicant will discuss medical problems with a physician more readily than with an agent, but the underwriter must not be lulled into a sense of security because of a completely satisfactory medical examination. Some people who are totally uninsurable because of a previous medical history may pass a medical examination. For example, a past history of heart attacks may not be readily detected by an examiner.

Paramedical examination. Sometimes instead of an examination by a physician, an insurer requires only a paramedical examination. A paramedical examination is conducted by a medical technician under the supervision of a physician and is a more economical way for the insurer to obtain detailed medical information. Paramedical examinations can also be easier for the applicant, as the organizations that provide them usually have accessible locations, convenient office hours, and, with medical technicians on duty at all times, easy availability of appointments. Another advantage of paramedical examinations is that they free physicians from the routine but time-consuming work of conducting insurance examinations.

A basic paramedical examination entails the completion of a form that includes the applicant's medical history, height, weight, pulse rate, blood pressure, and urinalysis results. This provides a considerable amount of useful medical information to the underwriter at a modest cost. If needed, other tests as well as a regular medical examination by a physician can also be conducted at the paramedical facility for an additional fee.

Attending physician statement (APS). If the application or medical examination discloses any serious medical condition or questionable history, the underwriter may ask for an attending physician statement (APS) from the applicant's regular physician. The APS gives detailed information on the applicant's current health and medical history, stating exactly what the applicant has been treated for, the dates and duration of treatment, and whether there was a complete recovery. It also provides information on any consulting physicians. The APS is the most complete and accurate source of information on medical history.

An example of the use of the APS: An applicant admits receiving treatment for high blood pressure. His physician would be asked to submit an APS providing information about blood pressure readings recorded, medication prescribed, and the degree of control achieved.

Laboratory tests. Laboratory tests may be conducted as a routine part of a medical or paramedical examination, or they may be required because of information that emerged in those examinations or in an attending physician statement. Tests include urinalysis, blood chemistry analysis, electrocardiograms, vital capacity test, glucose test, blood sugar tolerance test, and X-rays.

Blood tests are particularly useful, as they provide information on a wide range of conditions for a reasonable cost. Blood tests reveal:

- elevated cholesterol and lipids, which often lead to strokes or heart attacks;
- liver abnormalities (which may also indicate the presence of alcohol addiction);
- drug use;
- diabetes;
- disorders of the kidneys; and
- the presence of the human immunodeficiency virus (HIV), which causes the acquired immune deficiency syndrome (AIDS). Since the advent of AIDS, blood testing has become a much more frequent requirement of applicants.

Blood tests do not, of course, reveal all medical conditions, but fortunately the other tests mentioned can often provide needed information. For example, nicotine is readily traceable in urinalysis and can indicate if the applicant uses tobacco, and electrocardiogram tracings provide information on heart disease.

Inspection report. Inspection companies specialize in conducting independent insurance investigations. These companies investigate applicants and submit a written inspection report to the underwriter covering such matters as the applicant's occupation, financial status, and health history. Inspection companies have a great deal of experience in this area (they have existed for nearly as long as the insurance industry itself), and inspection reports are valuable underwriting tools. Both inspection companies and insurers are aware of the privacy issues involved in such investigations and have established procedures to keep the information gathered confidential.

Income documentation. An applicant's income is relevant to the underwriting of disability income insurance. Therefore, applicants for this coverage must usually certify their annual income in the application or an attachment. They may also have to submit a copy of their latest income tax return. Self-employed persons may be required to file additional financial forms showing the profitability of their business over several years.

MIB, Inc. MIB, Inc. (formerly the Medical Information Bureau) is an association of more than 700 companies writing life and health insurance in the United States and Canada. This association manages an information exchange that member companies can use to obtain accurate information about applicants for coverage.

The information exchange works in the following way. MIB maintains a list of **impairments** (conditions or circumstances that might make a person a bad insurance risk). These are mostly medical conditions, but include some nonmedical impairments (such as a bad driving record). When a person applies to a member company of MIB for coverage, the company must report to the association any listed impairment that it discovers in the course of the underwriting process. If at a later date the same person applies to another member company for coverage, that company can check the database to verify that the person does not have an impairment that he is concealing.

MIB only records information discovered by member companies during underwriting—it does not employ investigators or obtain copies of records from agents, doctors, or hospitals. Furthermore, companies report only the existence of an impairment, not the type or amount of insurance applied for or whether the reporting company issued or refused coverage. Thus, information from MIB is useful, but limited. It primarily serves to alert underwriters that a problem may exist and that further investigation is necessary.

MIB also maintains the **Disability Income Record System (DIRS),** a similar information exchange for disability income insurance. When a member company receives an application for an individual disability income policy with a monthly benefit of $300 or more and a benefit period of 12 months or more, it reports this to DIRS, which stores the information for five years. Other member companies can access this information to ensure that an applicant is not overinsuring himself by getting coverage from more than one company. DIRS involves no medical information.

To qualify for full membership in MIB, an insurance company must have a medical director and sell life insurance. Consequently, some insurers specializing in health insurance cannot become members. On the other hand, any insurer that writes disability income insurance is eligible for an associate membership, which provides both DIRS services and MIB information for a disability application.

Individuals have the right to challenge the accuracy of any information reported to MIB.

Individual Underwriters and Sales Personnel

Supporting the field sales force is an important part of an individual underwriter's job. This involves maintaining close communication with agents and providing them with the information about the status of pending applications they need in order to deal effectively with clients and make sales. The timely processing of applications by underwriters is also important in helping agents make sales.

Summary

Like group underwriting, individual health insurance underwriting is concerned with accurately predicting claims so that sufficient premiums can be charged to pay for those claims. Unlike the group underwriter, however, the individual underwriter examines the specific circumstances of the person or persons to be covered. She looks at their present and past health to determine the likelihood of future claims. In the case of disability income insurance, she also looks at their financial situations. She must consider information from many sources in determining whether coverage can be offered to an individual and on what basis.

17 REINSURANCE AND REINSURERS

- *How Reinsurance Works*
- *The Advantages of Reinsurance*
- *Types of Reinsurance*
- *Technical Assistance Provided by Reinsurers*
- *The Health Reinsurance Field*

Introduction

Just as an individual or business uses an insurance company to manage a risk, an insurance company itself may use another insurance company to manage and share risk. This is known as reinsurance. This chapter will explain how reinsurance works and what its advantages are.

How Reinsurance Works

Reinsurance means "to insure again." It works in the following way: An insurer issues a policy to an individual or business. That insurer then purchases reinsurance from a second insurer to protect itself against a part of the loss it may incur if it has to pay claims on that policy. That is, if the individual or business suffers a loss and the first insurer has to pay claims, the second insurer has to reimburse the first insurer for a part of those claims.

There are many types of reinsurance agreements. One example: An insurer issues a comprehensive major medical policy with an overall maximum benefit of $2,000,000. It arranges for another insurer to accept the second million dollars of that risk. This means that the first insurer will be responsible for paying all claims made by the policyholder up to $1,000,000, but the second insurer will reimburse the first insurer for all claims over $1,000,000.

The insurance company that issues the original policy is known as the **direct-writing insurer** (because it is the entity that writes, or issues, the coverage directly to the policyholder) or the **ceding insurer** (because it cedes, or passes on, part of the risk to the other insurer.) The insurance company that agrees to accept part of the risk from the direct-writing insurer is the **reinsurer.**

The contract between the policyholder and the direct-writing insurer is unaffected by reinsurance—the direct-writing insurer still has the same obligation to pay benefits as before. The direct-writing insurer has simply made its own arrangements for obtaining the funds to meet that obligation. In case of loss, the direct-writing insurer pays the policyholder, and the reinsurer reimburses the direct-writing insurer. No contract exists between the policyholder and the reinsurer.

If the amount of reinsurance is large, the reinsurer may pass a portion of it to another reinsurer. This is called **retrocession**. A reinsurer retrocedes coverage for the same reason a direct-writing insurer purchases reinsurance, that is, to share and manage risk.

The Advantages of Reinsurance

Reinsurance transfers risk from the ceding insurer to the reinsurer. This means that the ceding insurer, instead of possibly having to pay a very large amount in claims at one time, pays small amounts of reinsurance premiums on a regular basis in exchange for protection against a large claim loss. In other words, reinsurance works for the insurer in exactly the same way that insurance works for an individual or business. This has a number of advantages:

- Insurers are protected from very large unexpected claim losses. This is especially important for small and medium-sized insurers who do not have the resources that larger companies do.
- By substituting regular reinsurance premium payments for large unexpected claim losses, insurers can avoid wide fluctuations in their profit/loss balance from year to year, making planning and orderly growth possible.
- By sharing risk, an insurer can accept business that it otherwise would have to decline as too great a risk.
- By sharing risk, an insurer can experiment with new coverages that it might otherwise consider too risky, and so be innovative and maintain competitiveness.

Types of Reinsurance

There are two major types of reinsurance arrangements:

- In **automatic reinsurance,** an agreement, called a treaty, is made between an insurer and a reinsurer. They agree that all risks of any policy the insurer issues, provided they meet certain criteria (for example, all risks over $100,000), will be ceded by the insurer and accepted by the reinsurer.
- In **facultative reinsurance,** risks are handled on a case-by-case basis. In other words, the insurer can ask to cede any risk to the reinsurer, and the reinsurer can accept or reject any risk.

Technical Assistance Provided by Reinsurers

In addition to helping insurers manage risk, many reinsurers also provide insurers with technical assistance. A reinsurer's personnel usually have extensive knowledge and experience in the insurance field and can provide expertise in many areas including claims, administration, technology, actuarial science, product development, and market analysis. The most important area where reinsurers provide support is underwriting. Underwriting support includes:

- classifying occupations;
- assisting in the underwriting of difficult cases;
- recommending whether changing medical and nonmedical requirements is feasible;
- providing training for underwriters through seminars; and
- supplying underwriting manuals for insurers that do not have their own.

In cases where a reinsurer works with an insurer on a regular basis, the two companies often develop a very close relationship. A reinsurer's technical assistance can be particularly important to a small insurer or to an insurer new to the field.

The Health Reinsurance Field

The health reinsurance field is a relatively recent development compared to life reinsurance. This is because reinsurance is most needed when the maximum amounts that insurers might have to pay on policies are high, and before the 1960s these amounts were fairly low for health insurance. At that time, however, maximum benefit limits for disability income and major medical policies were raised substantially. As a result, even the largest health insurers began to share risk with reinsurers and the health reinsurance market began to develop. Nevertheless, there are still more life reinsurers than health reinsurers.

Summary

Insurance companies buy reinsurance from other insurance companies as a way to manage risk. Reinsurance protects insurers from very large unexpected claims losses and helps them avoid wide fluctuations in their profit/loss balances. It allows them to accept business that they otherwise would have to decline as too high a risk and to experiment with risky new coverages. Thus reinsurance enhances the financial stability, growth, and innovativeness of the insurance industry.

18 HEALTH INSURANCE PAST, PRESENT, AND FUTURE

- *The 19th and Early 20th Centuries: The Emergence of Modern Health Insurance Coverages and the Beginnings of the Health Insurance Industry*

- *The Great Depression, World War II, and the Growth of Employment-Based Health Insurance*

- *The 1950s and 1960s: The Modern Health Insurance Environment Takes Shape*

- *Recent and Current Trends*

Introduction

In this book we have examined how health insurance works, the types of companies that make up the health insurance industry, the different kinds of coverages offered, common contract provisions, and the procedures and techniques used in sales, marketing, and underwriting. In this final chapter we will look at how health insurance and the industry are changing. But first, to ensure a clearer understanding of these changes, we will learn how early coverages and companies developed into the health insurance industry of today. This is followed by a survey of the current trends that are affecting us today and shaping the way we will protect against illness and injury in the future.

The 19th and Early 20th Centuries: The Emergence of Modern Health Insurance Coverages and the Beginnings of the Health Insurance Industry

Most people think of health insurance as a modern development. But in fact, since the beginning of civilization people have made arrangements to avoid financial loss because of an accident or illness. For example, in ancient China people paid their doctor while they were well and in return the doctor treated them without payment when they were ill. During the Roman Empire a form of insurance provided income when an accident prevented someone from working. Similar arrangements existed in Europe in the Middle Ages, and beginning in the 17th century there were laws providing sickness insurance for seamen and dismemberment insurance for soldiers. Thus, simple forms of insurance providing some protection have existed for centuries. However, the modern system of health insurance that has been described in this book, with its array of coverages and sophisticated techniques, began in the 19th century.

Early Accident Insurance

In the mid-19th century, English railroads suffered from bad publicity because of accidents, and railroad management sought a means of alleviating the public's fear of train travel. In 1848, the Railroad Passengers' Assurance Company of London was established to deal with this problem. This company issued the first travel accident insurance. Passengers bought this insurance in the form of an extra stub on their railroad ticket, and in the event of severe injury or accidental death during that trip, they (or their heirs) received a lump-sum benefit. The Railroad Passengers' Assurance Company soon expanded its activities to insure all types of accidents, and other companies followed, both in England and in the United States.

Sickness Insurance

Another early form of health insurance was sickness insurance. Sickness insurance was not the same as modern medical expense insurance, which reimburses the insured for the actual medical expenses she incurs. Sickness insurance was more like disability income insurance, in that it paid a pre-set amount (or a pre-set amount per day) if the insured fell ill, and this benefit was intended not only to pay medical bills but also to compensate for lost income due to inability to work.

The first sickness insurance was issued in the United States in the mid-19th century, about the same time as the first accident insurance, but this coverage did not become widespread until the 1890s. Even then, the policies issued were very limited. For example, Fidelity Life and Casualty issued a combination accident and sickness policy under which only 15 specified diseases were covered, no benefits were given for the first seven days of illness, and benefits ended after no more than 26 weeks.

Companies limited coverage in this way because at that time there were few reliable statistics on the frequency of illnesses. This lack of information made it difficult for companies to accurately estimate the likelihood of a person falling ill, and so it was very difficult for them to know how much they were likely to pay in claims and how much they should therefore charge in premiums in order to be able to pay those claims without going bankrupt. Given this situation, companies tried to guard against the possibility that they would have to pay a very large amount in claims by issuing these very restricted coverages. However, as companies gained more experience and gathered more information, they were able to liberalize policies, which eventually covered all diseases and surgical procedures, eliminated waiting periods, and extended the maximum time period of benefits.

Group Insurance

These early coverages were sold as individual policies. The first group health insurance policy in the United States was written in 1910, when Montgomery Ward and Company arranged for an insurer to provide weekly benefits for its employees who were unable to work because of sickness or injury. During the following years many large insurers began to sell group health insurance plans to employers and groups.

Problems of the Early Health Insurance Industry

In the late 19th and early 20th centuries, the business of both accident and sickness insurance grew rapidly. Many new companies were formed, and existing fire and life insurance companies entered the accident and sickness field. However, the new industry faced a number of problems:

- Competition was intense, and in response many companies cut their premium rates so low that they could not make a profit.
- Despite some progress, companies still had insufficient information and experience to accurately predict the incidence of illness and so determine how much premiums should be to cover the costs of claims. Consequently, even those companies that made every effort to charge adequate premiums often miscalculated and lost money.
- Also due to insufficient experience, many companies accepted applications for insurance that they should have refused as bad risks. As a result, these companies paid more in claims than they received in premiums.

These circumstances caused many companies to lose money and go out of business, which hurt those insured by them and damaged the industry's reputation for reliability.

The lack of adequate information for underwriting caused yet another problem. Although, as mentioned above, some liberalization of policies had occurred, many companies still tried to reduce their risk by issuing policies with many restrictions. Often these restrictions were hidden in the fine print. As a result, situations arose in which an insured expected certain benefits based on his understanding of the policy but in fact the company had no obligation to pay those benefits. Although in such cases the companies usually were legally within their rights as stipulated by the fine print of the policy, the credibility of the industry was damaged in the eyes of the public.

Early Government Involvement

Due to the environment of intense competition, there were few cooperative efforts among insurers to solve the problems of the industry. The result was that state governments stepped in. State licensing and regulation of insurance had begun in the 19th century, but both legal requirements and supervision by regulators were very limited. This changed with the Armstrong Investigation of 1905. This investigation into the practices of life insurance companies resulted in greater government involvement in all kinds of insurance. Many states enacted new statutes that dictated the provisions of insurance policies and governed the operations of insurers. States also made efforts to more closely supervise the industry to ensure that it was complying with statutes and regulations. A landmark statute of this period was the Standard Provisions Law. This model law, designed to make the operating provisions in health insurance contracts more uniform, was developed by the National Convention of Insurance Commissioners in 1912 and adopted in 27 states.

The Great Depression, World War II, and the Growth of Employment-Based Health Insurance

The Great Depression of the 1930s devastated the health insurance industry. Millions of people lost their jobs and had little money to pay for "extras" like insurance, so few bought new policies and many stopped paying the premiums on their existing policies. In addition, many people falsely claimed sickness disability benefits, since these benefits were sometimes the only possible source of income for someone who could not find a job. As a result, the claims that companies paid rose in relation to the premiums they received. The common problems cited above (lack of underwriting information, insufficient premiums, and acceptance of high risks) meant that many companies were already financially shaky, and in the face of this drastic decrease in business, many failed. Other companies withdrew from the health insurance field, and still others offered only extremely limited policies.

However, as damaging as the Depression was, there were many positive developments during this period. Companies became more financially cautious, which helped bring about a more stable industry with fewer company failures. Also, a new spirit of cooperation emerged—companies became more willing to share with each other information about the claims that they paid, and actuaries and underwriters were able to use this information to set premiums at competitive but adequate levels. Finally, medical expense insurance, which had been pioneered in the 1920s, developed and spread, and employment-based group health insurance, on which the modern health insurance environment is centered, emerged.

The Development of Medical Expense Insurance

Medical expense insurance differs from the earlier sickness insurance in that benefits take the form of reimbursement for the actual cost of hospital, surgical, and medical services, not a lump-sum payment for days of illness. The first form of medical expense insurance was individual hospital expense insurance, which was written in the 1920s. This insurance covered only hospital services (not surgeons' or physicians' services) and was first offered by hospitals themselves. The first group hospital expense insurance policy was written in 1929. Baylor University Hospital in Dallas, Texas insured 1,500 school teachers who were members of a mutual benefit society. The benefits provided were up to 21 days a year of semiprivate room and board and necessary hospital services and supplies.

During the Depression, hospitals were faced with declining revenues as people without jobs could not afford to pay for hospital care. As a solution, many hospitals adopted the group hospital expense insurance plan pioneered at Baylor. Many people who could not pay large hospital bills could pay small premiums, and these premiums provided the hospitals with income. Eventually, around the country several hospitals in the same state or part of a state banded together to offer this kind of insurance. This was the origin of the Blue Cross plans.

Group hospital expense insurance was also provided by employers and commercial insurers. This first occurred in 1934, when the General Tire & Rubber Company asked its insurer to add hospital expense benefits to the group insurance program it provided for its employees.

Hospital expense insurance covered only services provided by hospitals, not surgeons' fees nor physicians' charges for hospital, home, and office visits. This gap was filled when commercial insurers introduced group surgical expense benefits beginning in 1938, followed by group medical expense benefits to cover physicians' visits in 1943. Physician-sponsored surgical-medical coverage was first offered in 1939, when the state medical society in California established the California Physicians' Service, a statewide plan. This was the first of the Blue Shield surgical-medical plans.

The Spread of Employer-Sponsored Group Health Insurance

Employer-sponsored group health insurance plans (which centered on medical expense coverage) experienced tremendous growth in the 1940s. This growth was spurred by war-time wage controls, labor union demands, and tax policy.

During World War II, in an effort to control inflation, the federal government prohibited industrial employers from raising wages or prices. This meant that although labor was scarce because so many people were in the military, employers could not raise salaries to attract and retain workers. But providing fringe benefits, including health insurance, was not forbidden, and this is what many employers did.

Labor unions have been active in the United States since the mid-19th century, but before the Depression only a small minority of workers were union-members. In the 1930s and 1940s unions grew dramatically and gained increased leverage in negotiating with employers. One of the things that unions began to demand was employer-sponsored group health insurance, and in 1948 the National Labor Relations Board ruled that unions had a right to make this demand as part of collective bargaining. The Supreme Court confirmed this ruling in 1949. As a result, employment-based group health insurance became the norm for unionized labor. Most unionized companies offered group health insurance to their nonunion managerial employees as well.

The growth in employment-based group health insurance was also encouraged by federal tax policy. Employers were allowed to deduct as a business expense their expenditures for employee health coverage. And individuals did not have to pay income tax on employment-based health coverage—even though it was given to the employee by the employer it was not considered taxable income. This made health insurance attractive to both businesses and employees.

The 1950s and 1960s: The Modern Health Insurance Environment Takes Shape

In the decades following World War II, the United States fully recovered from the Depression and entered a long period of prosperity and dynamic economic growth.

The health insurance industry grew rapidly as well, with many new companies forming and existing life insurance companies entering the health field. Unions negotiated group health plans with employers, and many nonunionized employers also provided group health insurance to their employees. Many new coverages were developed. State regulations were revised, and the federal government established programs for the poor and the elderly. As a result, a health insurance environment emerged with the following features:

- Most people get their health insurance through an employment-based group plan.
- A wide variety of coverages are available.
- Government takes a role as a regulator and in providing for certain populations.

This is essentially the health care environment that we have today—the major difference is the current importance of managed care.

New Products

The growth of health insurance during this period was due in part to the booming economy, as well as to the continued effects of tax policy and labor union pressure. However, this growth was also a result of the development of new coverages, which made health insurance more attractive to consumers.

Perhaps the most important new product was major medical coverage. The basic medical expense coverages developed during the 1930s did not cover prolonged hospital stays and expensive procedures. To provide protection against such events, in 1949 the Liberty Mutual Insurance Company introduced major medical insurance to supplement basic medical expense insurance. An illustration of the impact of this new product: a typical early medical expense plan covered a hospital stay of only 21 days at a limited amount per day and provided a maximum surgical benefit of $200 to $300; the new major medical policies typically covered an unlimited number of hospital days and reimbursed for surgical and medical expenses up to a maximum of $1 million or greater.

Other products introduced during this period were the following:

- comprehensive major medical insurance (combining into a single policy the previously separate basic medical expense and major medical coverages);
- dental expense insurance;
- credit health insurance (covering the insured's financial obligations, such as mortgage and car payments, in case of illness);
- long-term disability income insurance;
- vision care benefits;
- extended care facility benefits (for nursing home care);

- prescription drug benefits; and
- group plans for trade associations, professional associations, and multiple-employer trusts.

Government Involvement

State insurance regulations were updated during this period. The National Association of Insurance Commissioners (NAIC), which replaced the National Convention of Insurance Commissioners, developed the Uniform Policy Provisions Law (UPPL) in 1950. This model law, or the essence of it, was adopted by all states.

The federal government gained the power to regulate insurance, but decided to leave this responsibility largely to the states. The Supreme Court ruled in 1944 that insurance is interstate commerce, which the Constitution grants the federal government the right to regulate. Congress responded to this decision by passing the McCarran-Ferguson Act, which granted to the states the regulation of insurance. However, Congress has passed laws affecting insurance and has involved the federal government in the field by establishing government health care programs. The first of these, Social Security Disability Insurance (SSDI), was established in 1956, and the Medicare and Medicaid programs were begun in 1966.

Industry Organizations

In 1956 the Health Insurance Association of America (HIAA) was formed from the merger of two smaller industry associations that had existed for more than 50 years. This consolidation enabled the health insurance industry to broaden its activities in research and statistics and to provide more widespread dissemination of valuable industry information. HIAA also developed an extensive health insurance curriculum. (Recently, HIAA and the American Association of Health Plans joined together to form America's Health Insurance Plans, which represents 1,300 companies providing health insurance to over 200 million Americans.)

Other educational and training programs for the industry emerged in this period:

- The **Disability Insurance Training Council (DITC)** was established to conduct annual disability income clinics on university campuses.
- The **Chartered Life Underwriters (CLU)** program began to incorporate health insurance information.
- The **American College**, sponsor of the CLU program, introduced a health certificate course.
- The **Life Underwriter Training Council (LUTC)** began offering a special health insurance training program to be conducted at local levels.

Recent and Current Trends

Changing Demographics

The employment-based group health insurance plans of the 1940s and 1950s were designed to meet the needs of the traditional family—a male employee with a nonworking wife and two or three minor children. Today's work force and family structure are quite different, with more women working, fewer children per family, more single people, and more single heads of households. Insurers have developed new products to meet the different needs of people in different circumstances, so that the selection of coverages continues to expand. And employers have made it possible for people to choose among these coverages by offering flexible benefit plans.

Another important demographic change is that, since people are both having fewer children and living longer, the average age of the population is rising. This has caused an increased need for medical care, as will be discussed below, but it has also resulted in changes in insurance plans. For example, many employers are adding long-term care insurance and post-retirement medical insurance benefits to their group pension plans.

Consumerism

Consumerism, a powerful force in society since the 1960s, is a social movement supporting the rights and powers of buyers in relation to sellers. It is natural that the insurance industry should be a focus of consumer advocates, both because of the fiduciary nature of the business (the insurer is entrusted with the responsibility of acting in the interest of beneficiaries) and because it has such a great impact on the lives of so many people.

Some results of the consumer movement include:

- Insurers have developed coverages that provide benefits for alcoholism, drug addiction, home health care, mental and nervous disorders, newborn children, and handicapped children, and that provide for the continuation of survivors' health benefits.
- State laws have been enacted that mandate minimum health insurance benefits. Such laws require that certain types of coverage include certain benefits for certain conditions (including some of the conditions listed in the previous item).
- State laws have mandated confidentiality of medical care information.
- Federal legislation has been passed requiring that employers make continuation of coverage available for terminated employees.

Increasing Utilization of Health Care

Recent decades have seen an increase in medical services provided. Reasons include:

- **The rising average age of the population.**
- **Advances in medical science.** Scientists have continued to develop new and better ways to diagnose and treat health problems. Consequently, many people who before would not have received treatment, either because the cause of their ailment was not known or because no effective treatment existed, now receive medical care.
- **Greater availability.** The increase since World War II in the proportion of the population with health insurance and the growth in medical facilities have made health care available to many more people than before.
- **Greater awareness.** Health education by the mass media, the schools, medical societies, employers, labor unions, health insurers, voluntary agencies, and all levels of government has expanded public awareness of health matters and increased demand for medical care.
- **Catastrophic illnesses** such as the acquired immune deficiency syndrome (AIDS).

Increasing Cost of Health Care

The improvement in health and the extension of life brought about by the new treatments and diagnostic tools are among the great advances in modern civilization. However, as medical care has become more highly specialized and more dependent on expensive technology and drugs, the cost of that care has increased dramatically. In recent years, for example, the health care component of the Consumer Price Index has risen about twice as fast as the average of all goods and services. The increased utilization of health care and the higher cost of that care have led to higher health insurance claims and higher premiums for consumers. Insurers have responded to this problem in a number of ways:

- Aggressively controlling company expenses and improving efficiency and productivity.
- Improving underwriting to reduce losses.
- Requiring insureds to pay greater amounts in deductibles and coinsurance. (The greater the proportion of health care costs paid by the insured, the lower premiums can be.)
- Shifting to managed care, both by encouraging insureds to move to managed care plans and by introducing the cost-control techniques of managed care into

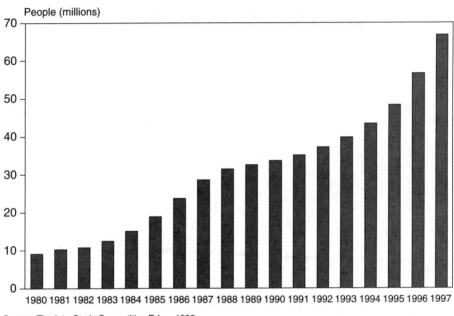

FIGURE 18.1

Enrollment in HMOs, 1980–1997

People (millions)

Source: The InterStudy Competitive Edge, 1998.

traditional insurance. This is the approach that has had the greatest impact. (See Figure 18.1.)

An Increasing Number of Uninsureds

After several decades in which the proportion of the U.S. population covered by health insurance rose, there has lately been a disturbing development—the number of uninsured people has been increasing substantially. This number reached an estimated 44 million by 1998. There are several causes for this trend, including the erosion of Medicaid coverage for the poor and the movement of more workers into part-time, temporary, and service sector employment, which typically does not provide group health insurance. But the most important cause is the increasing cost of health care, which has led to higher premiums and made employers less able to provide group insurance and individuals less able to pay premiums for either group plans or individual policies. Laws mandating that certain coverages

FIGURE 18.2

Persons with Employer-Sponsored Health Insurance and Uninsured Persons, 1988–2002

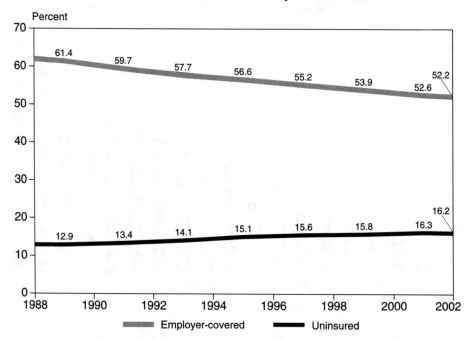

Note: Employer coverage includes workers and dependents with employer-sponsored coverage and retirees whose employer-based retiree benefits are their primary source of coverage.

Source: The Lewin Group. Estimates based on data reported in the March Current Population Survey for 1988 through 1994, adjusted to reflect the changes in survey methodology in 1995. Projections are based on trends reported from 1988 to1994.

include certain benefits have also contributed to the problem by making those coverages more expensive. (See Figure 18.2.)

Increased Competition

The health insurance industry has become highly competitive in recent years. This has had the following results:

- To stay competitive, insurers have had to continually develop new products, concepts in coverage, and funding vehicles. These innovations provide improvements and alternatives for consumers.

- Service has become a major competitive factor in the group insurance field. An insurer's ability to provide high quality service is increasingly important in obtaining and retaining group policyholders. High quality service means effective communication, sound administration, adequate computer capabilities, and prompt, accurate payment of claims.
- Some insurers are negotiating discounted contracts with hospitals and physicians. Such arrangements give an insurer a significant cost advantage over its competitors.

Mergers and acquisitions. Another result of competition has been the dramatic increase in mergers of health insurance companies and acquisitions of one company by another. Mergers and acquisitions can make companies more competitive in the following ways:

- They create larger companies. Large companies have certain competitive advantages, such as economies of scale. In a mature market (that is, a market for a well-established product that is not experiencing significant sales growth), mergers and acquisitions may be the only way to dramatically increase the size of a company.
- They enable companies to move quickly into new areas with high growth potential by merging with or acquiring companies that already have operations in those areas.
- They allow companies to focus on their most profitable areas of business by selling off peripheral areas to other companies who are seeking acquisitions. Many insurers have realized that they do not have the resources to remain competitive in all areas of insurance. They have identified product lines in which they have expertise and a competitive advantage, focused their resources there, and divested themselves of peripheral product lines. Acquisition strategies by other companies make this divestment possible.

Much of the recent merger and acquisition activity has been among mutual companies. They have been at a competitive disadvantage compared to stock companies, due to the greater capacity of stock companies to raise capital. In fact, many mutual companies have been faced with a choice: tap into the capital market (by converting to stock ownership) or merge. Some mutual companies have both converted and merged, as conversion to stock ownership facilitates merger by allowing one company to buy the stock of the other.

The shift to managed care is an important factor in the increase in mergers and acquisitions. This occurs in several ways.

- Traditional insurers move into the managed care market by merging with or acquiring managed care organizations.
- Managed care organizations move into product lines new to managed care (such as workers' compensation and disability insurance) by merging with or acquiring companies specializing in those areas.

- Strong managed care organizations acquire smaller managed care organizations in an effort to increase their presence in a particular geographical area.

Joint ventures. Joint ventures are another way of improving competitiveness. In a joint venture, an insurer forms a relationship with another company in order to do something better or to do something it could not do alone, such as provide a service or product or reach a certain market. Joint ventures have been part of the insurance industry for a long time, but there has been a proliferation of new types in recent years, including:

- **outsourcing** of certain functions such as administration, investment, or underwriting to other insurers or specializing firms;
- **alliances** between North American insurers and start-up companies in other countries, particularly developing countries; and
- **private labeling**, whereby a better known company sponsors and puts its name on the product of a less well-known company. This is common for specialty products, such as long-term care and disability income insurance.

The fast pace of change in today's insurance industry can make it difficult for an insurer to keep up with developments in all product lines. Joint ventures are one way for an insurer to continue to offer several lines by making use of the expertise of other companies.

Summary

The health insurance industry in the United States has enjoyed a history of steady and sometimes dramatic growth and development. This is because the industry has continuously improved its products to better meet the needs of the public and developed its techniques and organization in response to economic, social, and political changes. This tradition of progress and innovation continues today, as the industry meets the challenge of solving problems such as rising health care costs and the increasing number of uninsureds. The industry will continue to grow and change, and it will continue to fulfill its role of providing businesses and individuals with protection and financial security.

INDEX

Accident insurance (early), 160–161
Accident medical expense insurance, 38
Accidental death and dismemberment insurance (AD&D), 36–38, 67, 74, 132, 137, 145
Accumulation period, 26, 31
Acquisition expenses, 108, *131*
Acquisitions. *See* mergers and acquisitions.
Activities of daily living, 49–50
Actuaries, 114, 157, 163
AD&D. *See* accidental death and dismemberment insurance.
Administrative services only (ASO) arrangement, 13, *17*
Advances on commissions, 109, 111
Adverse selection, 56–57, 76, 125, 127, 130–131, 136–138, 144
Advertising, 19, 116–117
Age (in underwriting), 125, 127, 132–133, 140, 144, 147
Agencies, 10, *89*–90, 100–101, 110–111
Agents, 12, 64, 68, *89*–91, 94–112, 114–116, 118, 123, 140, 146–147, 152
Aging of population, 8, 52, 167–168
Aleatory contracts, 62-*63*
All cause deductibles, 26

All conveyance business trip AD&D, 37
Alliances (among insurers), 172
All-risk business trip AD&D, 37
Amendments to contract, 65
American College, 166
Annuity contracts, 6
Anti-selection. *See* adverse selection.
Any-occupation definition of total disability, 45–46
Application for insurance, 60-*62*, 64, 68–69, 74, 81–82, 93–94, 103–104, 117, 146–149, 152
Approach (sales), 102, 104
Armstrong Investigation, 162
ASO. *See* administrative services only arrangement.
Assets of insurance companies, 9–10, 18
Assignment of benefits, 71
Associations, 5, 48, 73–75, 77, 81, 115, 118, 166
Attending physician statement, 150
Automatic reinsurance, 157

Basic medical expense insurance. *See* hospital-surgical insurance.
Baylor University Hospital, 163
Beneficiary, 6, 86

Benefit (definition), 2
Benefit period, 34, 49
Benefit waiting period. *See* elimination period.
Billing, 94, 117, 120, 138
Blue Cross and Blue Shield Association, 16
Blue Cross/Blue Shield plans, 10, 13, *15*–17, 163–164
Bonuses, 112
Branch sales manager, 100–101, 112
Branch sales office, 100–101
Broker fees, 90, 112
Brokers, 12, 68, *90*, 92–100, 107, 112, 114, 116, 140
Business interest insurance, 48
Business trip AD&D, 37

Cafeteria plans. *See* flexible benefit plans.
California Physicians' Service, 164
Canadian insurance industry, 18–20
Cancellation, 84
Cancer insurance, 35
Capacity to contract, 60
Capital, 13
Casualty insurance, 5-7, 10, 12, 18, 95, 100
Ceding insurer, 156
Centers of influence, 102
Chartered Life Underwriters (CLU), 166
Claim (definition), 2
Claims provisions of contracts, 70–71, 86
Closing a sale, 93, 96–97, 103, 105
COB. *See* coordination of benefits.
COBRA. *See* Consolidated Omnibus Budget Reconciliation Act of 1985.
Coinsurance, 25, *27*–32, 34, 38, 40, 168
Cold call, 102

Commissions, 46, 48, 90, 100–101, *107*–112, 118, 120
Common carrier business trip AD&D, 37
Community rating, 16
Competition, 114, 125, 141, 156, 161, 170–172
Comprehensive business trip AD&D, 37
Comprehensive major medical, 21, *25*–26, 28, 155, 165
Conditional contracts, 62
Consideration, 60, 69
Consolidated Omnibus Budget Reconciliation Act of 1985 (COBRA), 78
Consultants. *See* employee benefit consultants.
Consumerism, 167
Contracts of adhesion, 62-*63*
Contracts, *2*, 19, *59*–87, 120, 135, 156
Contributory payment of premiums, 136–138
Conversion privilege, 78–79, 118
Coordination of benefits (COB), 71, 138,
Copayment, 32, 34, 39
Core-plus format flexible benefit plans, 55
Corridor deductibles, 27
Cost illustration, 92–93
Cost of health care, 54, 168–169, 172
Cost-of-living adjustment, 47
Coverage (definition), 2
Credit health insurance, 165
Credit life insurance, 6
Creditor groups, 115
Critical illness insurance, 35

Deductibles, 25, *26*–32, 34, 38–40, 114, 168
Definitions (in contracts), 63–64, 85

Demographic changes, 8, 52, 132, 167–168
Demutualization, 14–15
Dental insurance, 7, 18, *29*–32, 74, 165
Dental services, 30–31
Dependents AD&D, 37
Dependents, 37, 50, 67-*68*, 71, 77–78, 81, 85, 132, 135–136, 140, 167
Depression. *See* Great Depression.
Direct mail marketing, 116-*117*
Direct sales, 38, *104*, 116
Direct writing insurers (reinsurance), 156
Direct writing insurers (sales), 95
DIRS. *See* Disability Income Record System.
Disability buy-out insurance, 48
Disability income insurance, *8*, 18, *43*–48, 52–53, 67, 74, 103, 109, 115, 118, 123, 132, 145–146, 151–153, 158, 160, 162, 165–166, 171
Disability Income Record System (DIRS), 152
Disability Insurance Training Council (DITC), 166
Dividends, 12, 14, 114
Doctrine of reasonable expectations, 63

Effective date, 72, 75–76, 82–83
Eligibility date, 75–76
Eligibility for coverage, 135–136, 140
Elimination periods, 45, 49, 82, 161
Employee benefit consultants, 90, 92, 95–96, 114, 116
Employee Retirement Income Security Act (ERISA), 140
Employment in insurance, 9–10, 12, 18
Endorsement of contract, 65
Enrollment cards, 74–76, 93–94, 140

Enrollment of insureds, 74–76, 93–94, 96–97, 137
Entire contract clause, 68, 85
Equitable sharing of risk, 4
ERISA. *See* Employee Retirement Income Security Act.
Evidence of insurability, 76, 130, 137
Exclusions and limitations, 23–25, 32–34, 36, 45, 50, 85, 130
Execution of contracts, 64–65, 94, 97
Experience pooling, 129
Experience refunds, 77, 92, 130
Extended benefits, 139

Facultative reinsurance, 157
Family and Medical Leave Act of 1993, 78
Family deductible, 27
Federal disclosure reports, 140
Fictitious groups, 131
Fidelity Life and Casualty, 160
Field sales office, 91, 94
Field underwriting, 99–100
Financial Services Modernization Act of 1999, 121
Financial status of applicant, 143, *146*–147, 151, 153
First-dollar coverage, 26, 38
Flexible benefit plans, 53–57, 167
Franchise plans, 116, *117*–118
Fraternal societies, 10, *17*
Fraud, 60, 62, 84–85, 114
Fringe benefits for agents and brokers, 90, 101, *111*–112
Full-flexible format flexible benefit plans, 55–56
Fully contributory payment of premiums, 109, *137*
Functional capacity, 48, *49*–50
Future increase option, 47

Gender (in underwriting), 125, 127, 132, 140, 144

General agency, 101
General agent, 101, 110
General Tire and Rubber Company, 163
Geographical variations, 22, 30, 133
Good faith, 60
Government programs, 10–11, 18–19, 24, 38–41, 47, 50, 103, 111, 165–166, 168
Grace period for payment of premiums, 69–70, 85–86
Great Depression, 162–164
Group insurance (definition), 5, 73
Group insurance markets, 114–116
Group life supplement AD&D, 37
Group representatives of insurers, 90–97, 112, 140–141
Group service representatives, 90–91, 96
Guaranteed insurability option, 47
Guaranteed issue, 130
Guaranteed renewable policies, 83–84, 86, 118

Hazards, 1–2, 92, 145
Head office. *See* home office.
Health Insurance Associate (HIA), 166
Health Insurance Association of America (HIAA), 166
Health Insurance Portability and Accountability Act of 1996 (HIPAA), 24, 84, 128, 130, 139, 144
Health Maintenance Organizations (HMOs), 13, *16*–17, 139
HIA. *See* Health Insurance Associate.
HIAA. *See* Health Insurance Association of America.
High-low commission schedule, 108–110
HIPAA. *See* Health Insurance Portability and Accountability Act of 1996.

Home health care, 8, 34, 39, 43, 48–50, 52, 167
Home office of an insurer, 91–92, 94, 96, 119, 123, 140
Hospital charges, 21–22
Hospital expense insurance, 163
Hospital indemnity insurance, 34, 117
Hospital room and board expenses, 21–22
Hospital-surgical insurance, 21–25, 28, 118, 165

Impairments, 146, *151*–152
Income of insureds, 44–48, 54, 133, 138, 140, 143–147, 151
Income protection insurance. *See* disability income insurance.
Incontestable clause, 85-*86*
Individual Accident and Sickness Insurance Minimum Standards Act, 85
Individual insurance (definition), 5, 81
Inflation, 47, 50–51, 164, 168
Inspection reports, 140, 151
Installation of plan, 94, 96–97, 109
Insurance companies (number), 6, 10, 18
Insured (definition), 2
Insurer (definition), 2
Insuring clause, 70
Integrated deductible, 27
Integrated dental plans, 30
Internet, 116, 118, 121
Interview (sales), 102–104

Joint ventures, 65, *172*

Key-employee disability income insurance, 48

Labor Management Relations Act of 1947, 115

Labor unions, 5, 73–75, 77, 81, 92, 109, 115, 136, 164–165, 168
Laboratory tests, 21–22, *150*–151
Late applicant, 76
Late entry, 76, 137
Level commission schedule, 108–110
Liability (definition), 13
Liberty Mutual Insurance Company, 165
Life insurance, 3, 5-6, 9–10, 12, 18, 35, 37, 53, 73, 100–101, 111, 151–152, 157–158, 161–162, 165
Life Underwriter Training Council (LUTC), 166
Limitations. *See* exclusions and limitations.
Lines of coverage, 73–74, 95
Long-term care insurance, *8*, 24, 43, *48*–52, 67, 74, 103, 121, 137, 165, 167
Long-term disability insurance. *See* disability income insurance.
Look-back period for preexisting condition, 23–24
Loss of time insurance. *See* disability income insurance.

Mail-order prescription drug programs, 33
Major medical insurance, 21, *25*–28, 103, 118, 155, 158, 165
Managed care, 10, *16*–17, 54, 114, 134, 139, 165, 168–169, 171–172
Managed Healthcare Professional, 166
Mandated benefits, 121, 167, 169–170
Manuals. *See* rating manuals *and* underwriting manuals.
Market analysis, 120, 157
Market research, 119
Mass marketing, 102, 104, *116*–118
Maternity and pregnancy, 22–24, 45
Maximum benefit periods, 34, 45, 82, 161

Maximum benefits, 30–31, 36, 145, 158. *See also* overall maximum benefits.
Maximum indemnity amount, 44
McCarran-Ferguson Act, 166
Measurability of loss, 3
Medicaid, 11, *18*, 166, 169
Medical examination, 147, 150
Medical expense insurance, *7, 21*–28, 30, 33–34, 38, 43, 53, 67–87, 109, 117–118, 123, 132, 145, 160, 163–165, 167
Medical history, 60, 82, *145*–146, 150–153
Medicare supplement insurance, 38–41
Medicare, 18, 38–41, 78, 166
Meeting of the minds, 60, 63
Mental/nervous disorders, 24, 50, 167
Mergers and acquisitions, 16, 65, 171–172
MHP. *See* Managed Healthcare Professional.
MIB, Inc., 151–152
Military health insurance programs, 18
Minimum enrollment requirements, 75, 135–137
Minimum premium plan (MPP), 13, *17*
Model laws, 84–87
Model Life and Health Insurance Policy Language Simplification Act, 85
Modular format flexible benefit plans, 54–55
Montgomery Ward and Company, 161
Monthly or weekly indemnity (disability income insurance), 44, 46
Morbidity, 48
MPP. *See* minimum premium plan.
Multiple employer trusts, 114, 166
Mutual companies, 10, *14*–19, 124, 171
Mutualization, 15, 19

NAIC. *See* National Association of Insurance Commissioners.

National Association of Insurance Commissioners (NAIC), 84–85, 166

National Convention of Insurance Commissioners, 162, 166

National Labor Relations Board, 164

Negotiated union-management trusteeships, 115

Noncancellable policies, 83, 86

Noncontributory payment of premiums, 74, *136*–137

Nonintegrated dental plans, 30

Nonoccupational AD&D, 37

Nonrenewable for stated reasons only policies, 83

Nonrenewal, 84

Nursing home care, 8, 39, 43, 48–50, 52

Occupation of insured, 87, 132–133, 140, 143–145, 151, 157

Occupational accidents and illnesses, 24, 132–133, 144–145

Offer and acceptance, 61, 65

Official Guide for Filing and Approval of Accident and Health Contracts, 85

Optional contract provisions, 59, 87

Optionally renewable policies, 83-*84*, 118

Ordinary life insurance, 6

Outpatient charges, 22

Outsourcing, 172

Overall maximum benefits, 22, 25, 28, 31, 34–36, 38, 155

Overhead expense insurance, 47–48

Overinsurance, 71, 138, 152

Override commissions, 110

Own-occupation definition of total disability, 45–46

Paramedical examination, 150

Per cause deductible, 26–27

Permanent life insurance, 6

Persistency, 109, 131

Personal insurance, 5–6

Personal producing general agents (PPGAs), 101

Physical condition, 145–147, 150–153

Physician's inhospital charges, 22

Plan design, 56, *91*–92, 116, 137

Plan specifications, 92–93

Policy (definition), 2, 61–62

Policyholder (definition), 2

Portability, 50, 78, 167

PPGAs. *See* personal producing general agents.

PPOs. *See* preferred provider organizations.

Pre-approach letter, 102

Preexisting conditions, 23–24, 45, 50, 86, 130, 138–139

Preferred provider organizations (PPOs), 16, 139

Pregnancy and maternity, 22–24, 45

Premium (definition), 2

Premium cost sharing, 135, *136*–137

Premium provisions of contracts, 69

Prescription drug insurance, 32–33, 166

Primary insurance policy, 103

Primary interim need category, 103, 116

Primary permanent need category, 103, 116

Principal sum (AD&D), 36–37

Private labeling, 172

Probationary waiting period for coverage, 75–76, 103

Product design and development, 120, 157

Product development statement, 119–120

Product introduction, 120

Product outline, 119–120

Profit, 12–14, 17, 48, 114, 124–125, 151, 161

Proof of loss, 86

Property insurance, 5-7, 10, 12, 18, 95, 100

Proposal. *See* sales proposal.

Prospecting, 91, 96–97, 101–102, 104

Pure risk, 5

Railroad Passengers' Assurance Company of London, 160

Rating manuals, 127, 129, 139

Record-keeping in group plans, 74–76, 93, 138

Referrals (sales), 101-*102*, 104

Regulations (agents and brokers), 19, 89–90

Regulations (availability of individual insurance), 144

Regulations (Canada), 19–20

Regulations (cancellation), 84

Regulations (commission schedules), 108–109

Regulations (confidentiality), 167

Regulations (Consolidated Omnibus Budget Reconciliation Act of 1985), 78

Regulations (continuation of coverage), 78, 167

Regulations (contracts), 59, 63–65, 120

Regulations (conversion privilege), 78

Regulations (effective date), 82–83

Regulations (Employee Retirement Income Security Act—ERISA), 140

Regulations (exclusions), 24, 86, 130

Regulations (Family and Medical Leave Act of 1993), 78

Regulations (Financial Services Modernization Act of 1999), 121

Regulations (fraternal organizations), 17

Regulations (fully contributory plans), 137

Regulations (group legal definition), 118

Regulations (Health Insurance Portability and Accountability Act of 1996—HIPAA), 24, 84, 128, 130, 139, 144

Regulations (history), 162, 164–166

Regulations (Labor Management Relations Act of 1947), 115

Regulations (long-term care personnel and facilities), 50

Regulations (mandated benefits), 121, 167, 169–170

Regulations (maternity and pregnancy), 22–24

Regulations (model laws), 84–87

Regulations (mutual companies), 14–15

Regulations (no loss-no gain), 138–139

Regulations (ownership type change), 14

Regulations (preexisting conditions), 24, 86, 130

Regulations (premium rates), 127, 144

Regulations (small group underwriting), 126, 130–131

Regulations (stock company formation), 13

Reimbursement plans (prescription drugs), 32

Reinstatement, 86, 109

Reinsurance, 155–158

Reinsurers, 156–158

Reliability of claims data, 134

Renewal of coverage, 65, 69, 83–84, 94, 108–110, 114, 127, 135, 137, 139

Representations, 62

Request for proposals (RFP), 91–92, 140

Rescission, 60, 62, 85

Research and development, 119–121

Residual disability, 45–46

Retrocession, 156

Return of premium option (disability income insurance), 47
Revision of contracts, 65, 68, 127
RFP. *See* request for proposals.
Rider to contract, 65
Right of examination, 82
Risk (definition), 5
Risk management, 1–2

Sales incentives, 111–112
Sales monitoring and review, 121
Sales proposals, 91-*92*, 96–97, 117
Schedule of benefits, 82
Selection against the insurer. *See* adverse selection.
Self-billing, 138
Self-inflicted injuries, 3, 24, 36, 45, 50
Self-insured groups, 10, 13, *17*, 95
Service plans (prescription drugs), 32–33
Short-term monthly indemnity coverage, 46
Sickness insurance, 160–161, 163
Single employers, 114
Small group market reforms, 130
Social insurance substitute, 47
Specified disease insurance, 35–36
Speculative risk, 5
Standard Provisions Law, 162
Stock companies, 10, *12*–17, 19, 171
Supplemental insurance, 7–8, 24-25, *29*–41, 43, 103–104, 116, 118
Supplemental major medical, 21, 25, 27–28, 74
Supplemental need category, 103, 116
Supreme Court, 164, 166
Surgical charges, 22–23
Surgical schedule, 22–23, 30
Surplus, 13–15, 124

Taft-Hartley Act. *See* Labor Management Relations Act of 1947.

Taft-Hartley groups. *See* negotiated union-management trusteeships.
Taxes, 15–17, 19, 46, 151, 164–165
Ten-day free look provision, 82
Term life insurance, 6
Term of contract, 65
Termination of a group member's coverage, 77–78, 139
Termination of a policy, 70, *72*, 75, 77, 83–84
Terms of coverage (definition), 124
Third-party administrators, 33, *95*, 112
Third-party sponsorship, 116-*117*
Time Limit on Certain Defenses Provision, 85–86
Total disability, 44, *45*–48
Trade associations. *See* associations.
Training allowances for agents, 111–112
Training of agents, 90–91, 96, 100–101
Travel accident insurance, 38, 104, 160
Treaty (reinsurance), 157
Twenty-four-hour AD&D, 37

Unassigned benefits, 71
Uncertainty of loss, 3, 23–24
Underwriting manuals, 120, *126*–127, 157
Underwriting, 4, 48, *62*, 64, 74, 82, 92, 99–101, 117, 120, *123*–153, 157, 161–163, 168, 172
Uniform Policy Provisions Law (UPPL), 85–86, 166
Unilateral contracts, 62
Uninsureds, 11, 169–170, 172
Unions. *See* labor unions.
UPPL. *See* Uniform Policy Provisions Law.

Vesting, 110
Vision care insurance, 7, *33*–34, 165
Voluntary AD&D, 37

Waiting periods. *See* elimination periods *and* probationary waiting period for coverage.

War, 24, 36, 45

Whole life insurance, 6

Workers' compensation, 18, 24, 47, 132, 171

Worksite marketing. *See* franchise plans.

World War II, 164, 168

AHIP'S COURSES AND PROFESSIONAL DESIGNATIONS

For more than 40 years, the Insurance Education Program of America's Health Insurance Plans has offered current, comprehensive, and economically priced courses for professionals seeking to gain a greater knowledge and understanding of the health insurance industry. Since 1958, more than 500,000 people have enrolled in these courses. Many are employees of health insurance plans, but consultants, third-party administrators, agents, brokers, and other health insurance professionals also study with us. In addition, many noninsurance professionals, including health care providers, economists, consumer advocates, and government officials, take AHIP courses to learn more about the operations of our industry and advance their careers in their own fields.

Courses include:

- The Fundamentals of Health Insurance (two courses)
- Medical Expense Insurance
- Supplemental Health Insurance
- Managed Care (five courses)
- Disability Income Insurance (three courses)
- Long-Term Care Insurance (four courses)
- Health Care Fraud (three courses)
- Employee Health Care Benefits (two courses)
- Medical Management (six courses)
- HIPAA Rules, Requirements, and Compliance (two courses)
- Customer Service

The completion of AHIP courses leads to widely respected professional designations:

- Health Insurance Associate (HIA®)
- Managed Healthcare Professional (MHP)
- Disability Income Associate (DIA)
- Disability Healthcare Professional (DHP)
- Long-Term Care Professional (LTCP)
- Health Care Anti-Fraud Associate (HCAFA)
- Employee Healthcare Benefits Associate (EHBA)
- Medical Management Associate (MMA)
- HIPAA Associate (HIPAAA)

- HIPAA Professional (HIPAAP)
- Healthcare Customer Service Associate (HCSA)

Health Insurance Associate (HIA®)

The HIA® designation, offered since 1990, is held by more than 19,500 professionals. It signifies that the holder has acquired a broad knowledge of health insurance products and health plan operations. Designees have a solid understanding of insurance principles and terminology, contracts, underwriting and pricing, sales and marketing, policy administration, claims administration, cost management, regulation, and health care fraud and abuse. They are familiar with a variety of health coverages, including medical expense insurance, disability income insurance, long-term care insurance, and supplemental products such as hospital indemnity coverage, specified disease insurance, Medicare supplements, accident coverage, and dental plans.

Managed Healthcare Professional (MHP)

The MHP designation was established in 1996, and there are now more than 6,300 designees. Professionals with the MHP are knowledgeable about the latest developments in health care management as well as the operations of traditional health insurance. They have acquired an understanding of the structure and operation of managed care organizations, provider contracting and provider relations, network administration, member services, claims administration, and quality assurance, as well as marketing, rating, financing, and budgeting. They are also familiar with regulatory policies and processes, the accreditation of managed care organizations, and the role of health care management in government health benefit programs.

Disability Income Associate (DIA)

Holders of the DIA designation have an in-depth understanding of how an injury or illness can lead to a substantial financial loss and how disability income (DI) insurance can protect against this risk. Designees are knowledgeable about employer-sponsored disability programs, ranging from sick leave benefits to long-term disability income plans, and about federal and state government disability programs, including Social Security Disability Insurance, workers' compensation, and state temporary disability income programs. They also understand how individuals can supplement these employer- and government-sponsored programs with private DI insurance. Finally, DIA designees are familiar with the role DI insurance plays in retirement, estate, and long-term care planning.

Disability Healthcare Professional (DHP)

In the DHP designation program, students move beyond the specialized course of study of the DIA program to expand their understanding of the health insurance industry. DHP designees have the same in-depth knowledge of disability income (DI) insurance as DIA holders, including employer-sponsored benefits, government programs, individual DI policies, and retirement, estate, and long-term care planning. But they also have a familiarity with the principles of insurance, other health coverages, and the role DI insurance plays in the larger health insurance field.

Long-Term Care Professional (LTCP)

The LTCP program is an exciting opportunity for insurance professionals who want to learn about the increasing need for long-term care, the various ways of financing it, and the growing role of long-term care insurance. Students in the program learn about long-term care services, settings, and providers; they explore financing options such as personal savings, government programs, reverse mortgages, and annuities, discovering the limitations of each; and they examine in detail long-term care insurance, including policy provisions, underwriting and pricing, sales and marketing, policy administration, claims administration, and regulation. LTCP designees have the expertise they need to succeed in this expanding field.

Health Care Anti-Fraud Associate (HCAFA)

The HCAFA program provides those working in health insurance plan anti-fraud units and others with the information and skills they need to detect and prevent health care fraud and abuse. HCAFA designees understand how common fraudulent schemes work and how they can be discovered and investigated. They are familiar with many types of fraudulent activity, including fraud perpetrated by providers, consumers, agents, and health plan employees, as well as fraud involving a wide variety of health coverages, including medical expense insurance, managed care, disability income insurance, long-term care insurance, and others. Finally, holders of the HCAFA designation are knowledgeable about the laws and enforcement tools that can be used to stop fraud.

Employee Healthcare Benefits Associate (EHBA)

In the face of increasing medical costs, American workers continue to seek convenient and affordable health insurance coverage through their employers. Most employers want to provide an attractive benefit package while holding down rising costs in order to effectively meet the challenge of intensifying competition from both here and abroad. Legislators have recognized this challenge and taken steps to help employers meet it. The result is an expansion of benefit planning options that employers can combine in different ways to meet the needs of their employees. Those pursuing AHIP's EHBA designation gain an in-depth knowledge of these options and combinations, including how each of them operates, what benefits it provides to both employees and employers, and what regulatory requirements and tax treatment apply. Students also learn how a number of trends— greater employee mobility, longer life spans, an increasing need for long-term care, and rapidly rising prescription drug costs—have changed the environment of retiree health care and related benefits, and they explore the ways employers are addressing these changes.

Medical Management Associate (MMA)

The MMA program is designed for employees of health insurance plans who seek a deeper understanding of medical management and its impact on the insurance industry, as well as for health care providers, third-party administrators, and others whose businesses and practices are affected by it. The six courses of the program cover in depth the main branches of medical management: utilization management, case management, disease management, quality management, and call centers. Students also learn about legislative and regulatory requirements and accreditation and certification, and they explore emerging trends in this rapidly evolving field.

HIPAA Associate (HIPAAA)

The HIPAA Associate designation signifies that a person has acquired a basic working knowledge of the administrative simplification provisions of the Health

Insurance Portability and Accountability Act of 1996 (HIPAA), with a focus on the Privacy Rule. The program covers HIPAA terminology; organizational roles and responsibilities; policies and procedures; required documents, such as the privacy notice, business associate agreement, and authorization; patients' and individuals' rights; and guidelines on uses and disclosures of protected health information. By expanding their knowledge of compliance issues and HIPAA's impact on business and clinical practices, those earning the HIPAAA designation will be better positioned to help their organizations develop the policies and procedures required by this complex law.

HIPAA Professional (HIPAAP)

The HIPAA Professional designation is for those who plan to assume the role of HIPAA privacy official. As with the HIPAA Associate program, students learn about the policies, procedures, and documents required by the Privacy Rule as well as the rights of individuals and guidelines for the use and disclosure of information. HIPAAP designees supplement this basic grounding with more detailed study of HIPAA security standards and the measures that must be adopted to ensure the privacy and integrity of health data.

Healthcare Customer Service Associate (HCSA)

To stay competitive in today's environment, providers of health care services and products must offer outstanding customer service. The HCSA designation program helps people from all parts of the health care industry improve their relationships with internal and external customers and enhance the performance of their organizations. Students in the HCSA program acquire proven strategies for solving customer service problems; learn the basics of training, hiring, and managing customer service staff; and discover ways to achieve quality service and create customer-driven organizations.

For more information
visit our website (www.insuranceeducation.org)
or call 800-509-4422.

AHIP INSURANCE EDUCATION BOOKS

HEALTH INSURANCE

The Health Insurance Primer: An Introduction to How Health Insurance Works

This book, together with *Health Insurance Nuts and Bolts* (below), serves as a complete introduction to the health insurance field. The authors assume no prior knowledge and begin by explaining basic concepts and terminology, but they progress to an in-depth examination of such topics as the various kinds of health insurance, health insurance contracts, underwriting, and sales and marketing. *The Health Insurance Primer* is an excellent choice for beginners in the industry and those from other fields who need a basic understanding of health insurance. (Study manual included.)

Health Insurance Nuts and Bolts: An Introduction to Health Insurance Operations

The introduction to the fundamentals of group and individual health insurance begun in *The Health Insurance Primer* continues in *Health Insurance Nuts and Bolts*. Topics include policy issue, renewal, and service; claims administration; pricing health insurance products; managing the cost of health care; government regulation; and fraud and abuse. (Study manual included.)

Medical Expense Insurance

For those who have a basic grounding in the principles and functioning of health insurance, this book provides a more detailed look at the most common kind of health insurance in America—medical expense insurance. The text begins by describing the two coverages that provide health benefits to most Americans: group major medical insurance and individual hospital-surgical insurance. Subsequent chapters discuss contract provisions, underwriting and pricing, sales and marketing, policy administration, claims administration, and industry issues. (Study manual included.)

Supplemental Health Insurance

This book provides those with a basic understanding of health insurance and supplemental health insurance with more detailed information about the major supplemental products in the marketplace. These include hospital indemnity coverage, specified disease insurance, Medicare supplements, accident coverage, dental plans, and prescription drug plans. For each product, the text points out the gaps in basic health insurance that create the need for additional coverage and explains how the product meets that need and protects the individual from financial risk. (Study manual included.)

MANAGED CARE

Managed Care: What It Is and How It Works (Second Edition)

Completely updated and expanded by Peter R. Kongstvedt, MD, the foremost authority in the field, this book provides readers with a clear and easy-to-follow introduction to the fundamental concepts and basic functioning of health care management. It covers the origins and evolution of managed care, the various types of managed care organizations, network management, medical management, regulation, accreditation, and other topics. An extensive glossary of managed care terms is included. This book serves as the text for the AHIP course Managed Care, Part A. (Study materials available online.)

Managed Care: Integrating the Delivery and Financing of Health Care, Part B

The second book in AHIP's health care management series builds on the basic knowledge the student acquired in the introductory course, with a focus on operational issues and problems. It discusses in greater depth the governance and management structure of managed care organizations; selective medical provider contracting; network administration and provider relations; marketing and member services; claims administration; financing, budgeting, and rating; legal issues; accreditation; and regulation. (Study manual included.)

Managed Care: Integrating the Delivery and Financing of Health Care, Part C

Part C of this series explores a variety of topics. It describes the continued evolution of health care management, including the impact of regulation and consumer attitudes. It examines the role managed care plays in government health benefit programs, such as Medicare, Medicaid, and health benefit plans for federal employees and military personnel. The functioning of managed care in specialty areas, such as pharmacy, dental, behavioral health, and vision benefits, is discussed. Finally, ideas are offered on how the operations of managed care organizations can be improved. (Study manual included.)

PPO 101: A Comprehensive Overview of the PPO Industry

Preferred provider organizations (PPOs) have become a large and fast-growing segment of the health care financing industry. This book, offered in conjunction with the American Association of Preferred Provider Organizations (AAPPO), provides a solid grounding in this complex, dynamic, and expanding field. The reader learns how PPOs are organized and financed, what services they offer, what benefits they provide, how they are marketed, and how they compare with competing plan types. Many other topics are examined, including the various types of PPOs, the development and maintenance of a provider network, provider relations and reimbursement, customer service, quality management, and accreditation.

Dental Benefits: A Guide to Dental PPOs, HMOs, and Other Managed Plans (Revised Edition)

In this expanded and updated edition, Donald S. Mayes provides a comprehensive survey of managed care in the field of dental benefits. He explains how managed dental benefit plans function and how they differ from medical managed care plans. He describes the structure of managed dental plans, with a focus on the two main types, dental PPOs and HMOs. Several other topics, including cost issues and plan management, are discussed, and tools for evaluating and comparing dental plans are provided. This book serves as the text of an elective course in the MHP designation program.

DISABILITY INCOME INSURANCE

Disability Income Insurance: A Primer

Many people are unaware of the major financial loss that can result from a long-term disability, or they mistakenly believe that government programs will cover this loss. This book analyzes the financial risk of disability; it describes Social Security disability insurance, workers' compensation, and other government programs and makes clear why they do not provide adequate benefits for most people; and it explains how disability income (DI) insurance *can* provide sufficient benefits. Employer-sponsored group DI coverage is briefly described (it is fully covered in the third book of this series), while individual DI insurance is examined in detail, with a focus on underwriting, contract provisions, and claims administration. (Study materials incorporated into text.)

Disability Income Insurance: Advanced Issues

The second book in the AHIP disability series explores more complex issues, including structuring DI benefit programs to meet the needs of lower, mid-tier, and higher-level employees; combining group and individual DI coverage; implementing executive bonus and salary continuation plans; and coordinating DI insurance with both tax-qualified and nonqualified retirement plans. Specialty products, such as disability overhead expense insurance, key-person DI insurance, and disability buyout insurance, are described. Students also learn about the important role of DI insurance in planning for retirement, long-term care needs, and estate protection. (Study materials incorporated into text.)

Disability Income Insurance: Group and Worksite Issues

Many people look to their employers as the source of disability benefits, and many employers choose group disability income insurance as the best means of providing these benefits. In this book, the reader finds comprehensive and up-to-date information on all aspects of group DI insurance, including product design and policy features, underwriting and pricing, sales and marketing, and claims administration. A related product, voluntary worksite plans, is also examined, and regulatory and tax considerations are discussed. (Study materials incorporated into text.)

LONG-TERM CARE INSURANCE

Long-Term Care: Understanding Needs and Options (Second Edition)

As people live longer and the population ages, there is an increasing need for home health care, assisted living, nursing home care, and other forms of long-term care. This book provides an introduction to the field of long-term care and long-term care insurance (LTCI). It begins with an explanation of what long-term care is, who needs it, and how and where it is provided. It then looks at several ways of paying for long-term care and the limitations of each. It examines long-term care insurance, describing how it works and explaining why it is often the best solution to the problem. Finally, it discusses the ways salespeople and insurance company personnel can bring this solution to the people who need it. (Study materials incorporated into text.)

Financing Long-Term Care Needs: Exploring Options and Reaching Solutions (Second Edition)

Long-term care services can be very expensive, and if they are required for more than a few months the total cost can represent a significant financial burden. But by planning ahead, the average person can provide for his or her long-term care needs. This second volume of AHIP's long-term care series examines in greater detail the various ways of meeting the need for long-term care. It looks at personal savings and assets, family support, Medicaid, reverse mortgages, commercial and private annuities, life insurance, and both individual and group long-term care insurance. The advantages and disadvantages of each of these is discussed, giving the reader a clear understanding of the role each can play in long-term care planning. (Study materials incorporated into text.)

The Long-Term Care Insurance Product: Policy Design, Pricing, and Regulation (Second Edition)

Long-term care insurance (LTCI) is a relatively new and still evolving product. This book looks at this evolution, focusing on the innovations insurers have made to better meet consumer needs and on the impact of regulation, especially HIPAA. It also provides a comprehensive look at LTCI policies, covering benefit eligibility, benefit amounts, inflation protection, elimination periods, policy maximums, non-forfeiture, renewal, lapse, and other features. Other topics include premium calculation, group long-term care insurance, and the combination of long-term care coverage with other insurance products. (Study materials incorporated into text.)

Long-Term Care Insurance: Administration, Claims, and the Impact of HIPAA (Second Edition)

The administration of long-term care insurance continues to evolve as the product itself develops. This book looks at practices and procedures in several administrative areas, including underwriting, issuance, premiums, policy maintenance, policyholder services, and reporting. It describes the long-term care claim process and the steps insurers take to control claim costs and hold down premium prices. In addition, the impact of the Health Insurance Portability and Accountability Act of 1996 (HIPAA) is discussed. (Study materials incorporated into text.)

HEALTH CARE FRAUD

Health Care Fraud: An Introduction to Detection, Investigation, and Prevention

Every year, fraud and abuse add billions of dollars to our country's health care expenditures. This book describes how health care fraud is perpetrated and what is being done to combat it. It explains how some of the most common fraudulent schemes operate, how these schemes can be detected and investigated, and the laws that can be brought to bear against them. Fraud perpetrated by health care providers, consumers, and others is covered, and although medical expense insurance fraud is emphasized, fraud involving managed care and disability income insurance is also included. (Study materials incorporated into text.)

Insurance Fraud in Key Products: Disability, Long-Term Care, MedSupp, Drug Coverage, & Others

While the first book in AHIP's fraud series focuses on medical expense insurance, the second looks at a range of health insurance products: disability income insurance; long-term care insurance; dental, behavioral health, and prescription drug benefits; and Medicare supplement insurance. Fraud in two nonhealth coverages, life insurance and property/casualty insurance, is also discussed. For all of these products, common fraudulent schemes are examined, and legal and investigative issues are explored. (Study materials incorporated into text.)

Legal Issues in Healthcare Fraud and Abuse: Navigating the Uncertainties (Second Edition)

This book, written by Carrie Valiant and David E. Matyas and published by the American Health Lawyers Association, provides those working to combat health care fraud with the legal background relevant to investigations, civil actions, and criminal prosecutions. It surveys the major players in anti-fraud enforcement and examines in detail the most important laws and regulations. Topics include anti-kickback legislation, restrictions on physician self-referrals, false claims and fraudulent billing, exclusion from federal health benefits programs, fraud and abuse in managed care, state anti-fraud laws, legal representation issues, and many others. (Study materials available online.)

EMPLOYEE HEALTHCARE BENEFITS

Employee Healthcare Benefits: An Introduction to POPs, FSAs, HRAs, and HSAs

A variety of plans is currently available to employers seeking to provide their employees with an attractive package of health care benefits while holding down rising benefit costs. These plans—premium only plans (POPs), flexible spending accounts (FSAs), health reimbursement arrangements (HRAs), and health savings accounts (HSAs)—are the subject of the textbook for the first of AHIP's two self-study courses in employee health care benefits. The reader will learn how each of them functions, what features and advantages it offers, what potential drawbacks it has, what tax benefits it provides, and what regulatory requirements it must meet.

And coming soon, Book 2 in AHIP's EHBA program—Employee Healthcare Benefits: Funding Health and Related Benefits for Retirees.

MEDICAL MANAGEMENT

Medical Management: An Overview

The introductory text of this six-part series provides readers with a background in the development of managed care and an overview of its latest phase—medical management. Early models of managed care, current practice, and emerging trends are discussed. Readers learn why and how health care benefit plans are developed, how legislative and regulatory requirements affect the industry, and how accreditation and certification function to promote quality. (Study materials incorporated into text.)

Medical Management: Utilization Management

The purpose of utilization management is to determine whether health care services are medically necessary and appropriate. It seeks to ensure that the treatment, provider, and facility that best meet a patient's needs are chosen. This book describes utilization management's evolution and explores its future. The reader acquires an understanding of the goals of utilization management, the programs and organizations that have adopted it, the professionals who are responsible for it, the processes they use to implement it, and the tools and resources they need to support it. (Study materials incorporated into text.)

Medical Management: Call Centers

This book presents an overview of the "telehealth" industry—from standard call centers that serve health plan members to more sophisticated systems that provide access to registered nurses who can assist patients with specific health problems. Readers are given practical pointers on how to establish a call center, select vendors, hire and train employees, and maintain quality in customer service. They learn about legal and regulatory requirements and look at trends in the use of electronic communications in health care. (Study materials incorporated into text.)

Medical Management: Case Management

Case managers help patients and their families navigate health care delivery systems and manage their own health care needs. Practitioners come from many disciplines—they are nurses, social workers, rehabilitation counselors, and physicians—and they collaborate with other stakeholders to achieve quality, cost-effective outcomes. This book gives the reader a clear understanding of the basic concepts, goals, and processes of case management; the professionals and organizations in the field and the services they provide; legal, ethical, and risk management concerns; and emerging trends. (Study materials incorporated into text.)

Medical Management: Disease Management

Disease management is a system of coordinated health care interventions for a medical condition in which patient education and self-care are key components. This book takes a practical approach to the subject and offers plenty of substance to readers at all levels, from beginners seeking a basic understanding to managers of disease management programs. Topics include the history of disease management, current challenges, and future projections; model programs for specific diseases; the tools and techniques used in these programs; regulatory and legislative issues; and accreditation and certification programs. (Study materials incorporated into text.)

Medical Management: Quality Management

Providing the right health care at the right time in a way that produces the most favorable patient outcomes is the objective of quality management. This book covers the essentials, helping students understand why quality management is important, how programs are implemented, and who the key stakeholders are. It introduces students to the fundamental framework of quality management, providing an overview of the programs, processes, and procedures used by health care organizations to ensure the delivery of quality services. (Study materials incorporated into text.)

HIPAA

HIPAA Primer: An Introduction to HIPAA Rules, Requirements, and Compliance (Second Edition)

Who must comply with HIPAA? What does "protected health information" mean? What types of information must be protected? This practical guide to the Privacy Rule of the Health Insurance Portability and Accountability Act of 1996 (HIPAA) provides the answers to these questions and many more. It explains what the rule is, what its key components are, and whom it affects. It discusses key concepts such as covered entities, business associates, and the minimum necessary standard and offers examples of their real-life application. A glossary of HIPAA terminology is also included.

HIPAA Action Items for Insurers

This practical workbook provides clear guidelines that will help insurance company managers and personnel interpret the HIPAA Privacy Rule and implement compliance. It includes an easy-to-understand description of the essential elements of the Privacy Rule; an outline of compliance tasks, such as appointing a privacy official and training personnel; scenarios and case studies that show how HIPAA requirements apply in the insurance industry; and templates for creating compliance documents such as the privacy notice, business associate agreement, and authorization. (Study materials incorporated into text.)

CUSTOMER SERVICE

Customer Service Strategies for the Health Care Environment

In an easy-to-read style, this book offers strategies, tools, and exercises designed to make health care employees more aware of customer service issues and create a customer-driven organization. A wide range of topics is covered, including removing the barriers to excellent customer service; improving communication with customers; assessing the quality of customer service; analyzing service cycles; hiring, training, and managing personnel; and handling customer complaints. Many valuable resources are included, such as 50 expert tips for quality customer service and provocative self-study quizzes in each chapter. (Study materials available online.)

THESE BOOKS MAY BE ORDERED
BY CALLING 1-800-828-0111.

THE AHIP INSURANCE EDUCATION PROGRAM

Gregory F. Dean, JD, CLU, ChFC, LTCP
Executive Director

Joyce C. Meals
Deputy Director, Education

Norma Fleming
Accounts Coordinator—Registrar

Kevin Gorham
National Accounts Manager

Matthew Grant
Internet Services Coordinator

Charlene Burger
Administrative Assistant/CE Coordinator